# SLOW COMING DARK

# SLOW COMING DARK

## INTERVIEWS ON DEATH ROW

# DOUG MAGEE

The Pilgrim Press / New York

To Mom and Linda and in memory of my father

Copyright © 1980 The Pilgrim Press
All rights reserved

No part of this publication may be reproduced, stored in a retrieval system, or trans-
mitted in any form or by any means, electronic, mechanical, photocopying, recording,
or otherwise (brief quotations used in magazines or newspaper reviews excepted), without the prior permission of the publisher.

LIBRARY OF CONGRESS CATALOGING IN PUBLICATION DATA

Magee, Doug, 1947–
  Slow coming dark.

  Bibliography: p. 179–80
  1.  Death row—United States—Case studies.
2.  Prisoners—United States—Interviews.  I.  Title.
HV8699.U5M33     364.6'6'0922   [B]     80-19747
ISBN  0-8298-0400-5

James Agee and Walker Evans, *Let Us Now Praise Famous Men*, published by
Houghton Mifflin Company. Copyright © renewed by Mia Fritsch Agee. Reprinted
by permission of the publisher.
  Theodore Dreiser, *An American Tragedy* (New York: Signet Classics, 1973), p.
788.

The Pilgrim Press, 132 W. 31 Street, New York, New York 10001

# TABLE OF CONTENTS

In every child who is born, under no matter what circumstances, and of no matter what parents, the potentiality of the human race is born again: and in him, too, once more, and of each of us, our terrific responsibility towards human life; towards the utmost idea of goodness, of horror of error, and of God.

*Let Us Now Praise Famous Men*


Oh, if he could only go away from here—never to see or hear or feel anything more of this terrible terror that now hung over him. The slow coming dark—the slow coming dawn. The long night. The sighs—the groans. The tortures by day and by night until it seemed at times as though he should go mad.

*An American Tragedy*

# Introduction

"I would like Governor Graham to come see me. It seems to me that if he is to judge me he should know me. He cannot know me through papers or the words of my lawyers. That's just common sense. If he had investigated my case he wouldn't be doing this. If he's so sure of himself he wouldn't be afraid to come. I know who I am. I want him to know who he is killing—the real person, not some idea he has in his head about me.

That was a quote    (from John Spenkelink's last statement)

Just after ten o'clock on the morning of Friday the 25th of May 1979, John Spenkelink was wrestled from his cell in the Q wing of the Florida State Prison by six guards and carried struggling to a small room down the hall. His head and right calf had been shaved forcibly and he was gagged because he had shouted, "This is murder, this is murder!" In the center of the small room where he was taken was a three-legged oak instrument: the electric chair.

Wearing a white shirt with rolled up sleeves, Spenkelink was strapped into the chair at the arms, legs and chest. His mouth and chin were covered by a black muzzle wrapped tightly around his neck. A white towel, wrapped around his throat, secured his head to the back of the chair. The guards put a wet sponge on his head to conduct electricity better and then fitted a metal cap over the sponge. A black hood was drawn half over his head while the two black electrical cords that snaked out of a box on the wall behind the chair were connected to his body.

Before him he could see a plate glass window covered by a curtain running the length of the wall. To his right was an anteroom with a slit of window cut in the wall. Through the slit he could see two hooded men; one would be his executioner. The guards stood around the chair. The tight muzzle bulged his cheeks but he could see the movement of the curtain on the large window in front of him as it opened. He caught a brief glimpse of the witnesses behind the glass, as they did of him, before the hood was dropped quickly over his face.

Within seconds, what must have been horrible seconds for him, massive amounts of electricity jolted his body. Three doses in all. Smoke curled up from the burning flesh on the inside of his thigh and his fingers, gripping the flat armrest, curled backward in convulsion. He was dead.

I did not watch John Spenkelink's execution. I stood with the rest of the press in a fenced-in meadow across from the flat, green buildings of the Florida State Prison and listened first to the radio reports and then to the accounts of the witnesses and pool reporters. In the glare of a bright mid-morning sun I had trouble realizing that not more than three hundred yards from where I stood a man I had come to know in the eight months since I had first photographed him for a magazine article had been taken into an execution chamber and killed. As I listened to the details of his death his last statement played in my head like a broken record. His lawyers had to bring the statement out to the press; the prison authorities would not allow him to speak for himself. He said he wanted the Governor to come and meet him, to sit and talk with him like a human being. Many who heard those words thought they were preposterous. To me they sounded like common sense.

A cream-colored hearse carried John Spenkelink's body away from the prison. The big car sped into town and I looked past the line of state troopers, the big open field, the barbed wire and double chain-link fence to the prison. Those green buildings, swimming in the warm air of a late spring morning, stayed with me for days. The distance between us and the 133 other men left on death row seemed immense, unbridgeable.

I came to see the accuracy of that image. I realized, after looking into capital punishment more deeply, that the information we get about people on death row most often comes from intermediaries: lawyers, court records, journalists and social scientists. Like the people on death rows throughout the country, the people in the R and Q wings of the Florida State Prison are cut off from us and we from them.

Prison authorities say there are security reasons for this distance. I think it goes deeper than that. If the people on death row are allowed to speak for themselves, if they become human before us, we have to face the hard fact that we are executing human beings. The less we hear from them and about them the easier it is to pretend they are less than human. I failed John Spenkelink because I kept our acquaintance to myself. Soon after his execution I decided it was necessary to meet more of the nearly 600 other people on death row and to bring their voices and stories across the no-man's land that separates us from them. This book is the result of those conversations. It is my hope that the interviews and photographs in this book will introduce the reader to a part of our society that is closed off from public view, shrouded in a macabre mystery and romance, and is, in the main, misconceived by all but the most knowledgeable.

Though the only crime for which a sentence of death is given these days is aggravated first-degree murder, not all people convicted of such crimes are sentenced to die. All of the people now on death row can point to others not under sentence of death who have committed crimes similar to theirs. It is possible, perhaps even reasonable, to tolerate disparities and irregularities at many points in our criminal justice system. That system is, after all, a patchwork quilt dotted with idiosyncracies and not one smooth piece of fabric. But capital punishment is so final that we can't tolerate disparity or irregularity in its application.

In the twelve years that preceded John Spenkelink's execution the U.S. Supreme Court, through a series of rulings, tried to eliminate some of the worst inequities in the way we execute people in this country. If his execution is any indication, their efforts were a failure. Two men committed the crime for which John Spenkelink died. Spenkelink's partner turned state's evidence, served a short prison sentence and is now free. The execution that returned the death penalty from a twelve year hiatus was an exceedingly curious quirk of our judicial system.

Yet, as I researched this book, I found similarities in death penalty cases that seemed almost systematic. The practice of giving a light sentence to one of two people convicted of a capital offense in exchange for testimony and sending the other to death row is one. Another is that most people sentenced to die had minimal representation at their original trial. And almost all on death row are poor.

There is no mystery in this pattern. Representing a defendant on a capital charge is today one of the most difficult of all legal assignments. The trials are charged with the passion of outrage. The laws are confusing, complex and constantly changing. In these conditions the lawyer for the defense must be a cut above run-of-the-mill counsel and must have costly investigative resources equal to the prosecution's in order to keep the accused off death row. That quality of legal assistance is expensive. Those who don't have it are likely to lose. It is little wonder, then, that the vast majority of people on death row are poor. Almost all of them had to rely on public defenders and court-appointed lawyers who were overworked, inexperienced or without the funds for research and investigation that the prosecution could command. These people, when confronted with the greatest threat the law can offer, got less than adequate counsel.

We know the ideals of our legal system; we don't know the procedures. In our ignorance we may assume that a person who can't pay for representation is given legal assistance and resources on a par with those of the prosecution. That is rarely the case. With the return of routine executions in this country we will be sanctioning the killing of more and more people of a certain group: the poor. The forms will be observed. There will be many appeals and long delays. In the end, people who cannot afford adequate counsel will die. In our democratic society that is as unacceptable as executing the innocent.

Though most people might admit to ignorance of the way the death penalty is imposed in our judicial system, few doubt their own imaginative grasp of death row. The popular conception seems to be a mix of dungeon nightmare and James Cagney romance.

Death row in most state prisons is aptly named. A set of small, one-person cells, segregated from the rest of the prison population in some way, the typical death row is just down the hall from the electric chair or the gas chamber.

A death row cell is usually about six by nine feet and has three closed walls. The other, barred wall faces onto a corridor. A person inside a cell cannot see left or right of the cell. A mirror held outside the bars allows the inmate inside to see who is walking down the row. The room is ordinarily furnished like any other prison cell with a sink and an open flush toilet, a cot and a lightbulb. In some prisons the death row people are allowed their own televisions; in others there are wall-mounted TV's outside the cells, always on. The rest of the furnishings depends on prison rules and inhabitants. I saw no cell that looked comfortable. One, furnished only with a toothbrush, was the bleakest room I've ever seen.

4

Death row inmates are treated differently from the rest of the prison population. They are constantly in their cells. They have no work assignments around the prison and have the most minimal shower and recreation periods. For four days a week, on average, they spend all but ten minutes a day in their cells. On each of the other three days they have an hour out for "recreation," which is standing in a penned yard.

They are dependent on their guards for everything from food, toothpaste and stamps to communication with friends, family and lawyers. Because they are locked away with such totality they are virtually powerless to protest their conditions or even to make them known.

Death row is set up with one thing in mind: to hold a person until execution. None of the programs of education or rehabilitation available to others in even the strictest of prisons are available to death row inmates. The prison is required only to house, feed and then kill the inmate. This makes life on death row far more depressing and meaningless than life normally is in prison. During all my times on death row, I could not shake the feeling that I was standing in a ghastly zoo organized and wholly devoted to carrying out the most sordid act imaginable. That the people in the cells were accused of similar inhuman acts seemed not relevant. We have only institutionalized the killing we so deplore.

Near most death rows is a single cell used to prepare the condemned for execution and, close to that, the execution room itself. Because there had been a hiatus for the decade before these interviews were done, many of the electric chairs and gas chambers I visited were newly refurbished. The fresh coats of paint on the walls and the shiny new chairs in the witness rooms made it even harder to imagine that people were going to be killed summarily in these chambers. Texas, Oklahoma and Idaho have passed laws that mandate death in capital crimes by injection of a fatal drug. Presumably the aim is to reduce the horror by changing the means of execution. The effort misses the point. Read about

Of the death chambers I saw, two stand out in my memory as particularly odd, though all were eerie in their throne-like presentation of the death chair. In Alabama the electric chair was painted a bright, cheery yellow. In Arizona, behind the huge shiny gas chamber vault, in the witness room, are photographs of all the people who have been executed in the state. Those that were hanged have the nooses that killed them circling their pictures. That exhibit is perfect for prison tours. Like notches on a gunslinger's pistol, it displays a misplaced, sickening pride.

Death sentences used to be carried out in a matter of months after conviction. Now it takes years to execute someone who has been convicted and sentenced. Of course the legal precautions causing this delay are absolutely necessary; and yet as a side effect they make the death sentence even more terrifying than it was intended to be. Life on death row is just barely living. It is instinctive existence where the days are stitched together by a thin thread of hope that either the laws under which the penalty was decreed will be ruled unconstitutional or one's conviction will be reversed for some reason. The effects of years of isolation and deprivation, the lack of human contact, touch, and sexuality builds unrelievable pressures. The constant possibility of execution added to those pressures makes for a grinding, withering life that is all but intolerable—a "slow coming dark."

Reading and writing are the main outlets for death row tensions. Even the least literate of the people I met spent some of their time either writing letters or reading books that had been sent to them. In the interviews I did in the South the most mentioned book was the Bible. Most of these Bibles find their way to death row through evangelical ministries to prisoners. Many of the people I met on death row talked of their "Christian friends" who wrote to them. Some spoke about their own rebirth or conversion to Christianity. I'm sure many will scoff at these professions of faith as either affectations or conniving, on the *a priori* grounds that a person sentenced to die will do anything, including acting pious to escape execution. I don't choose to judge the sincerity of any of the claims of faith made in the following interviews. I assume that some do read the Bible and talk about religion because they hope it will help their case. And I assume some are truly full of faith. But I also assume that there is a group not in either of those categories for whom the Bible or letters from strangers who want to convert them to Christianity are like Gideon Bibles in motel rooms; lifesavers for the lonely, reading material that can be gone over often, correspondence with people who are concerned about you, something constructive to do. Death, of course, makes for seriousness. Anyone condemned to die might normally turn to the Bible or something like it, especially if there is religion somewhere in his or her background. But it seemed to me that the personal concern of these ministries, the letters, the suggestions to read the Bible, meant the most to the death row inmate who had little to do but sit and think about his own lonely death.

The bulk of interviews for this book were done in the southern states. As they were being conducted eighty-five percent of the 550 people under sentence of death were in those states. But the death penalty is far from a regional problem. As this is being written the northern states are following the South's lead, copying death penalty laws from states like Florida, Georgia and Texas which have had their statutes upheld as constitutional by the U.S. Supreme Court.

These interviews raise many questions that go unanswered. Points of fact are often left uncorroborated. Contradictions riddle some of the interviews. Were this book to be graded as an attempt to unravel the tangled string of events that some of these cases present, it would not get a passing mark. I have tried with all diligence to exclude obvious contradictions, to check assertions of fact before they were included, to edit the material so that as many questions as possible are answered. But the people in this book are, like all of us, complicated human beings. They have, for the most part, tried to make the jumble of their lives intelligible to me. When faced with the choice, I have included a rough, open-ended interview that is an accurate representation of a corner of death row instead of a tidy package that may answer all the questions while grossly misrepresenting the soul of the place.

The first interview in this book is anonymous. It was not originally intended to be so but the man's lawyer would not consent to the interview being published otherwise. Though my intent in publishing these interviews is to introduce the reader to specific people, the picture of death row given us by this man is invaluable to this book.

At the time they were interviewed all the people in this book were under an active sentence of death. It is only natural that we who meet these people have our suspicions. Reading these interviews we ask ourselves over and over whether those who are maintaining their innocence are innocent or guilty of the crimes for which they have been convicted. We haul out our sleuth selves or sit on an imaginary jury and try to crack the case, search for clues, catch up the criminal. Even those who admit guilt, we ask whether their remorse is sincere or whether we are being conned by someone who is desperate.

The crimes for which some of these people have been convicted are frightening and shocking; by virtue of their convictions we fear these people so much that our suspicions may never go away. I ask the reader to keep in mind, though, that this book is neither a murder mystery nor an appeal brief. It is simply an introduction to people who have been singled out by our criminal justice system and who are about to be put to death.

Not dealt with directly in these pages are the pain and suffering of the friends and families of the victims. Their plight is the subject for another volume. I did ask most of the condemned about the victims' friends and families. In most cases the people sentenced to death had had little to do with victims' families. This is reasonable, of course, given the fact that no restitution is possible.

In my research I did find one instance of an extraordinary exchange between a person on death row and the mother of that person's victim. I think it important to share it in this introduction though the interview is not included in this book.

Cardell Spaulding killed Roscoe Simmons with a homemade knife on the exercise yard at Central Prison in Raleigh, North Carolina. Convicted of the killing and sentenced to death, Cardell—who had been stabbed earlier by some of Roscoe's friends—thought he was just protecting himself when he struck out with his knife. The reason the interview I did with Cardell is not in this book is that after several years on death row Cardell received a new trial and his death penalty was reduced to life imprisonment.

While under sentence of death Cardell wrote a letter to Roscoe Simmons' mother saying he was sorry for what had happened and that he felt what he had done was in self-defense. With what must have been great difficulty, Mrs. Simmons replied. The substance of her letter follows:

Cardale,

I can't say how surprised I was to hear from you and I have taken my time in writing you back. I've asked God not to let me say any harm to you. I am a mother of two sons and two girls. I love them with all my heart. I rise them if they broke a house rule there was a price to pay. If they broke the law there was a price and most of all if they broke the law of God there was a big price and only they could pay it. I no you have a price to pay. If they kill you it won't bring my son back and it won't make my hurt hurt any less. But I'll tell you how I feel about you. Thank God I don't hate you. And I agree with you I feel the guard did have a part in Roscoe's death. But taking you at your word, you are the one who killed my son. You and you alone used the knife on him. Yes I no you almost die and I could have understood it if it was one of those boy you killed. But my son was a mile away. He had never done anything to you. And I no he alway went out of his way to make friends. He would have done all he could to get you all not to hate each other and make peace between you all.

Reggie has told me how Roscoe used to beg him not to hate you or any of the other boy. Because some day you would have God to answer to. And God only love what was good.

Cardale, Roscoe was not the first one you killed and I feel you would do it again if you had the chance. I can't ask them not to kill you yet I can't say for them to do it. I love your soul and I no your mother love you. You see I talk to your mother. I no she was hurting as I was. But she can go see you, put her arm around you. You no when I went to see Roscoe I only ask God to let me get my hand on my son one more time, not noing that one time would be in his casket. Now all I have to touch or look at is a grave. But I have asked God to forgive you for all this. I only pray you will ask him too . . .

I pray someday I'll meet you in heaven. I understand you have a child. Don't you no without God help I couldn't have wrote you this. I thank God for the love he has gaving me. I no someday I will be with Roscoe in heaven. I no those last minutes he live he ask God to save him and he's in heaven waiting for his mother.

Lucile<br>Roscoe Mother

Also not dealt with directly in these interviews are the arguments for and against the death penalty. Watt Espy's statement before the Judiciary Committee of the Alabama State Senate follows the interviews and covers some of those arguments. It is included in this book because, like the interviews, it speaks not of political, legal or ethical theories but of people: who gets killed and why. The historical record he has compiled gives a unique perspective on the human reality reflected in the interviews. It might even help some to read the statement before beginning the interviews.

All the people you will meet in these pages have been convicted of first-degree murder. The crimes for which they are on death row are some of the worst imaginable: the wanton, heinous, sick crimes that turn our stomachs and fill us with fear. Nothing about this book is an attempt to excuse these crimes. But my travels on death row have raised questions that I cannot shake.

The last interview I did for this book was perhaps the most disturbing of all. The man I talked with had killed three people for no apparent reason. He had turned himself in and confessed to the crimes after his brother had been falsely arrested. He had no jury trial and was quickly sentenced to death by a trial judge. The likelihood that he will be dead by the time you read this is great. As we spoke in the visiting room of a very secure prison, the full force of his sentence hit me. Here was a man who was caught, bound and immobilized securely away from society, a menace now to no one. We had done all that was needed to protect ourselves from this man and his violence. Anything further, his execution, seemed to have all the earmarks of the calculated, bloodthirsty violence we so detest in the very crimes for which he was condemned.

There is nothing that says we have to execute even the worst people in our society. Nothing surely that requires that we follow violence with violence, make them less than human and extinguish them. When we have done all we can to protect ourselves from their crimes, any added violence must be seen as patently offensive.

In the week before John Spenkelink was executed I had occasion to ask Florida's Governor Bob Graham whether he planned to meet Spenkelink personally. He said that he wouldn't and that he wanted to keep "emotion" out of his decision to sign the death warrant. I imagined then how necessary it must be for the people who sign death warrants and carry out the executions to objectify those they are putting to death. Because we all, to some extent, participate in the death sentences carried out in our name, we too must objectify those we have condemned. The path better taken, it seems to me, is that suggested by John Spenkelink's last words to the world. "I want him to know who he is killing—the real person, not some idea he has in his head about me."

# Anonymous

To this day he does not know how many people he killed. He knows he was responsible for at least eleven deaths in the fall of 1973. He has been questioned about a number of other murders that happened that fall in several western states and he speaks about killing two drug users in Phoenix in the summer of '73, but he has not been charged with any but the eleven deaths. In the course of five years on death row for the murder of a young couple, he has undergone psychiatric evaluation, hypnosis and drug treatment that have brought back many of the details of the crime spree that included the eleven murders. But he is still not sure how many people died by his hand.

He is, however, certain of one thing—that he is a sick man. He knows that he has had terrifying emotional problems for a long time and that these problems have at different times led him to the extremities of violence. He knows too that this lurking derangement is still with him and he is as afraid as society is that if he were given the opportunity, if he were even so much as taken off solitary confinement in prison, his sickness might lead him to kill again.

Thirty-four years old now, he was born and brought up, the youngest of three children, on a small farm outside of Lodi, California. He says that he was left alone a great deal as a child and did not get along well with his mother. His father, who suffered from a heart ailment of some sort, died when he was thirteen. The family then moved into a poor area of San Francisco and early in his teens he began to have trouble with school authorities and the police.

Though his mother had him examined for his emotional problems, he says she could not afford the therapy recommended by the examiners. He did time in juvenile institutions and as a young adult was sentenced to Vacaville, a California prison for the criminally insane. At one point in his late teens he enlisted in the Navy but was discharged when he could not abide by the authoritarian structure. His education was, of course, interrupted by his stays in institutions but he was able to study nursing at a minimum security prison in San Francisco in the late '60's.

Released from that prison in 1969, he married his cellmate's sister, worked as a nurse in a geriatric ward while studying for his R.N. and experienced a happy life for perhaps the first time ever. But his emotional problems, never really treated, caught up with him. He began using drugs, especially heroin, became irrational, paranoid and, at times, quite violent. There were periods, he says, when his violent side would erupt. He would attack his wife or friends, whoever was close at hand, and only later be aware of what he had done. Blackouts, perhaps caused by a head injury received in a motorcycle accident, became frequent. Finally he nearly killed his wife and, he says, fearing for her safety, he fled San Francisco in the late summer of 1973. His problem was no longer hidden.

In a six to eight week period he traveled throughout the country buying and selling drugs, robbing, beating and killing people wantonly, his last crime being the murder of a family of nine in their California farmhouse in 1973. The robberies, beatings and murders of that time were so littered with the mark of insanity and acted out with such total disregard for concealment that to call them the work of a sane or calculating mind stretches the definition of sanity beyond any intelligible limit.

He and his crime partner were arrested three days after the California murders and were eventually given life sentences. They were then extradited and were tried and convicted of the murders of a young couple. For those murders, he and his partner were sentenced to die in the gas chamber at the state prison. It was at that prison on two hot, dry summer days that he and I talked.

Five years on death row have changed him greatly. Photographs of him at the time of his arrest and trial show a wiry, clean-shaven man with a full head of bushy hair. Today he shows hardly any physical resemblance to those photographs. He is overweight now with closely cropped hair and a moustache. As he was being sentenced to die he defiantly asked the court to ignore his lawyer's plea for mercy: "I don't want any mercy, don't expect any and don't ask for any. I just want to get it over with as soon as possible." Today he speaks of his death sentence in more considered terms. He says he wants to fight his execution so that it will not be so easy for others on death row to be executed.

And he has come to understand more about himself than he ever had before. While he can't remember all the parts of the fall of 1973 he can at times walk the perimeter of that black hole and make some sense, at least for himself if not for us, of acts that are, in the end, horribly incomprehensible.

He is an intelligent man who speaks rapidly and forcefully. He unreeled his story and his thoughts about his life as if he knew that doing so would provide some release from the terrible images his memory brings him. At the painful parts of his narrative he remained dry-eyed and direct. But that seemed to me more an indication of style than of feeling. In the tumble of words and sentences the heartbeat of conscience, grief and guilt was unmistakable.

IT WAS IN '73 in about the middle of the year, in July or August. I think it was late July. I killed two men in Phoenix. They were drug users same as me. They were informers. We argued and I choked one to death and I beat the other one to death. And at that time I weighed about 135 pounds and was doing about $200 worth of heroin a day.

I left that time and nobody saw me for about four days. The police said there was another homicide during that four day period. I was never charged with it. I was questioned on it. I don't know whether I did it or not. But within a month and a half to two months of that time I had been involved in or been directly responsible for sixteen or seventeen homicides and between fifteen and twenty violent assaults without motives. One right in the middle of town in broad daylight. I just went crazy and started beating people on the streets, things of this nature. I would stop somebody and just beat them half to death and take their money. Maybe not even take their money. Just do it. And it escalated and escalated and escalated.

During this time, the police have told me, there was never any indication that I was trying to avoid arrest. I didn't hide or anything else. I just went my way, just like nothing had happened. I didn't try to get an assumed name. I didn't change cars. I didn't change my lifestyle. Why they didn't catch me, I don't know. I figure I just caught them by surprise. I had just completely run amok. I have a so-called crime partner. I don't really know whether he was ever involved in any of the crimes or not.

There's no doubt that I have brain damage. And the use of drugs at the time put me in a paranoid state to where I was afraid of everybody. I carried a gun and I used it. I'm sorry that it happened. I have a lot of remorse for that. But I can't actually remember walking in and saying 'I want to kill somebody' and shooting someone.

*But you take responsibility?*

Yeah, there's no doubt about my responsibility. I did use the gun on some people at one time for no reason. I mean there was no motive to it or anything. I was just paranoid and people were bothering me and these things would happen. I have no excuse for it.

The only thing in my favor was that I had tried to get psychiatric help before these crimes happened and had been turned away. It was not like this happened quick. It had built up over a year and I had tried and tried and tried to get help and I was turned away. I didn't have the money to go to a private sanatorium and I hadn't committed a crime, although I'd come pretty close to it.

Since then a lot of psychiatrists have come to interview me. Most of them, they just want to talk, see what happened for their own reasons, oh, they're writing a book or whatever. And I've probably gotten maybe twenty different reports from different psychiatrists. They all basically say the same thing: that I, at the time of the crime, was insane. And *now* there are times when I'm insane.

*Then something just sort of snaps, or was it the drugs you were doing at the time?*

Well I can't blame it on the drugs because that would be ridiculous. The drugs are more or less a symptom of whatever it is. . . . I've had emotional problems for a long time. In '73 I had an accident and it wasn't long after that when I started developing strange headaches. They'd get so bad I'd just black out.

I'd become different personalities, a complete different person. One person feels persecuted. All the hatred in the world comes on me. It gets pretty nasty and pretty ugly and there's nothing I can do to control it because it's real. Later on I can say, "Hey, well that's not real. I know these people. They weren't doing that to me." But at the time it's as real to me as anything in the world. And I would become extremely violent. I would come to myself two or three days later and be in San Francisco or somewhere and I wouldn't even know what had happened. My wife would try to talk to me about it and I wouldn't have any idea what the hell happened.

The headaches and blackouts got more frequent and more severe. It would happen almost in a dream fashion. It got to the point where I was really afraid I was going to hurt my wife or somebody else I cared for and so I left.

*Did you plead insanity?*

Yes, I did. We had psychiatrists there. The judge talked to them, but the jury never heard Dr. White. She said I was insane, explained what type of treatment I would need. The judge refused to let her testify to the jury. So I can't blame the jury because the jury didn't hear this and I wasn't up there trying to tell them I didn't do it.

I'm in a position where I wouldn't want to be released without care. Even releasing me out in the yard wouldn't make any sense because there are times when I'm paranoid, so paranoid, sick, just totally out of it that no one's safe around me. In this institution there is no way that I would get the help I need.

I'll never get out of prison. I don't care what they decide

on capital punishment. I am never going to leave an enclosed environment, a maximum security environment. Society never has to worry about me escaping or being turned loose next week or anything like that. I have fifty years minimum eligibility for parole. I'm 34 now so there's not too much chance that I would live even to meet my first parole board.

If in my case the death penalty is overturned they'll just put me out in the yard. The most they'll ever let you do is they'll give you a bunch of pills and keep you knocked out. Nobody wants to do that all the time. The psychiatrist doesn't want to do it to anybody all the time. Without it I become totally irrational, very violent, extremely violent. It's not safe to be around me.

Now I have to live with that every day. I have to live with the thought that I took several human lives. I did that. Nobody made me do it, nobody else did it. I did it and I have to live with those faces every night. I don't care what the reasons were behind it or how sick I was or anything else. I still have to live with that everyday and I'm not going to add to it, if you understand what I mean. I don't want to go out of here and freak out and kill some other guy who hasn't done a damn thing to me or anybody else, just walking in the yard minding his own business. Maybe some kid who's in here for possession of marijuana, three or four years for having one lousy joint of marijuana and some guy like me goes and freaks out and stabs him to death out here in the yard, chokes him to death or something. I have to live with that thought in my mind that this could happen at any time. It's a very, very frightening thing. I'm put in a position where it's either die in the gas chamber or take that chance. It's not right. It's not right at all. It's not fair to the other guys.

*Could you say a little more about the victims?*

I think about the victims constantly. I don't think there's anything in the world more repulsive or more wrong than to take another human life. I had no right, no one has a right to stop another person's life whether they're worthless or whether they're gonna be an Einstein. They had a right to live and I stopped it, just snuffed it out. And I live with that fact.

Every day I think about it. It hurts. It hurts a lot. We don't talk about it to the other guys down here. Most things you talk to the other inmates about is gallows-type humor because that's what keeps you sane. Insanity actually keeps you sane. But inside yourself you spend a lot of hours walking the floor and thinking about them, wishing to hell you hadn't done it. Not because you're here. Not because if I hadn't killed them I wouldn't be in prison. That has nothing to do with it.

But if they would release me tomorrow, if they were to give me a magic pill and make me perfectly normal and perfectly safe to society and release me tomorrow, I would still, every day of my life, live with the fact that I took a human life, wantonly, without provocation. There was no war situation. It wasn't a self defense situation. I just took it on myself to play God and I'll never forgive myself for that.

I truly think that if you talk to the guys down here and if they could bring themselves to be honest about it, they'd tell you the same thing. The few times they have, most of them have talked about it, they admit it. It's awful hard to admit it because you're living in a place where they want you to be strong. It's hard to survive in prison and to show something like that is to show weakness and it's not acceptable. But inside you've still got to live with it. Every night you go to bed with it. Every morning you get up with it. You shave with it, you eat with it and it eats at you.

I don't know how people out there feel. You watch TV and you see a lot of people get killed on TV. John Wayne dies five times a week. He gets up and goes home. In their minds that's what capital punishment is. They're gonna take us in a little room, they're not going to see it, they're going to drop a pill in us and it's no different from television. We're going to be dead but only in that sense.

And I guess I felt that way until the first person died of my hands. The one person you personally have killed. You know that person is never going to breathe again, he's never going to see the sky again, never going to see his children grow up. You're not going to forgive yourself for that. That's something you live with, not like stealing somebody's money. I don't suppose there's any way in words I can describe it. It's there and that is probably the hardest part.

*What is the punishment for that?*

There is no punishment! What could they do to me to punish me for what I did? That's a ridiculous concept. How do you punish me for taking a life? Take my life? That would punish me, I'm dead, my punishment ends right there. Believe me I've attempted suicide quite often. Death is no punishment, just the over and ending of it. If there is an afterlife then that's all there is. If there isn't, it's over anyway and you can't get anymore punishment than mine. I'm locked up in a prison. Beating me with a whip? That wouldn't change anything. That's just not going to change anything.

If people are really concerned, if they really are concerned about it, then they've got to keep people from doing it in the first damned place; got to try to get people young and special where they're not involved in situations like this prison, where they feel there's more value to making something than tearing it down. Got to give them a motive for living.

You can give a man a motive for killing very easily. A motive for living, a motive for getting up in the morning and going to work, a little self-respect and dignity is what's needed if people want to slow the crime rate. Now that's what they're going to have to do.

And they're never going to do it the way they're going. Build more prisons and they'll fill them up. It's that simple. They've been doing this. They've been having executions for God knows how long now and it's never slowed or stopped or done anything.

*There are a lot of people in this country who support the death penalty because they don't want their tax dollars spent to house and feed a convicted murderer for the rest of his life.*

Well they have a right to feel that way but their tax dollars are going to be spent for people in prisons whether they want 'em to or not. That idea, "Well, I don't want to spend the money so kill the guy," that's no better rationale than for me to say, "Well I don't want to work for a living so I'll just take your money." If you can find a motive for killing people, I don't care what your motive is, if you can find a motive for killing me and rationalize it to yourself, especially if that motive is that I'm costing you a little money, then what makes you different than the guy who wants your money so he kills you and your wife to take it? He had a motive, he rationalized it and he thought it was a good motive. So what makes him different than you?

You can always find a way to rationalize things if you want to put a dollar sign on it. But we're talking about human lives. We're not talking about automobiles. We're talking about another human being. And if they can put a price on it then they have no excuse for killing us in the first place, because if you can put a price on one man's human life, then you can't say I was wrong or anybody else was wrong for putting a price on someone else's life walking in the streets.

*But a law-abiding citizen will say, "I play by the rules. You can play by the rules."*

OK that's fine. You see you can always rationalize it and say, "Well, I'm a law-abiding citizen so you're wrong." OK I'm wrong. Make me believe it. Show me a way to function in society and help me do it and, by God, I'll turn around and help you

make a better life for yourself. But just by telling me I'm wrong and hitting me on the side of the head or throwing me in the gas chamber or locking me up in a little cage somewhere you're not going to make a friend out of me, or a helper. You're going to make an enemy out of me and not only am I going to be an enemy but a certain percentage of the people that I come into contact with are going to be persuaded that maybe they should be enemies of yours too.

Most people want to be accepted into society. Most people want to be liked and most people would be glad to go out there and do the right thing. They want to be liked by their fellow man and they would be damned well happy to work, do whatever it takes if they have the opportunity, if you show them the way.

*The word paranoia is used pretty loosely these days. You have used it to describe your mental state at times. Can you explain what the word means to you?*

Yeah. I can give you a perfect example of it. It's always the same. My family were Jewish and they had dropped the religion a long, long time ago. I married into a Christian family and I never, never mentioned to anyone that my family was Jewish. I started having those headaches and feeling everybody knew I was, you know, Jewish. They could see I was circumsized or something. I mean it was just like they knew it. And at the time I didn't want anyone to know. So I would get a little upset. I start feeling that people around me had tendencies to be Nazis. Then it reaches the point where they *are* Nazis. They truly are. I see that they are in human form. They are there and I react accordingly. I become irrational. There's no way anyone can talk to me.

I started getting that way with one of my cellmates. He thought it was kind of funny at first. I was telling him "You gotta watch these cops. These cops are Nazis, man. These guys have Nazi ideas in their heads and they're going to gas me because I'm a Jew and that's the only reason." This goes on for about three days and I got to the point where I wouldn't allow him to turn the television on because I thought they were monitoring us.

And then I got in a little locker and wouldn't come out for a day and a half. When I did come out, I came out hating the world. And every officer or inmate within reach was attacked. To me they were Gestapo and they were going to get me and that's all there was to it.

They had to keep me on prolixin for six months to bring me out of it. It comes to that point. It happens to me on the street. At the time I was arrested I did not realize this is what's happening. A lot of what I'm telling you is from the last five years of having time to think about it.

I was trying to treat myself with drugs, which were only making it worse because they were giving me more delusions. I would do some heroin and I'd be so bombed out that I couldn't move. So I'd do some cranks and methedrine on top of it and take some pills and maybe down a half a gallon of wine. Then I'd go out on the streets and by then everything was, you know, . . . the American flag had swastikas on it. No one could get near me. I'd be walking down the street and I'd just pull a gun and I would shoot because that was a Gestapo agent coming to get me. And it might be a mailman. Uniforms really did set me off. Any kind. The man I killed was a marine, a marine captain, and he was standing out in his yard wearing fatigues and evidentally that's what did it. I saw it, it set me off. I went in his house and by the time it was over, he and his wife were both dead.

*Were there any indications of this paranoia when you were very young? Did you grow up with your parents?*

Yes, with my parents. My father died when I was relatively young. I think I was 13. He was a very ill man for several years before that. That part was very unhappy. Both my brother and my sister are older. Most of my life was spent on the outskirts of a city, semi-country like until I was about 13. Then we moved into a situation, more of a ghetto situation, countrified ghetto. That's when I started having brushes with the law and with authority. Psychologists came up with all kinds of reasons. All I know is I just didn't like authority. But I never really had much trouble as a youngster.

*How was your schooling?*

Mediocre. I got by. That's about all I can say.

*You must have picked up some kind of education along the way.*

Yeah. When I got out this last time I attended junior college. Even when I was in prison this last time I decided that education was the only thing that was going to keep me out. So I studied and attended classes. The last year and a half, almost two years, I was in prison I was lucky enough to go into California's Men's Colony in San Francisco. It's sort of a model prison with a real good education program. I got a job with the education department. Part of the time I worked as a clerk and the other half I could go to classes and read on my own. I went to a junior college and studied nursing and I worked in a hospital. I felt pretty good about it. It was something I really enjoyed doing. I loved working in a hospital environment. I like to work with people like that and geriatrics is what I specialized in. This was the only time in my life I've had a sense of accomplishment: when I worked with mostly terminally ill old people. If I could make them have one day of feeling good, I would go home at night after 12, 14 hours and would just feel great. My entire day was made. It didn't bother me at all.

It's probably the only thing in my entire life that I can actually say I'm proud of. I really enjoyed it and I felt I did some good there. If this thing hadn't have happened, I'd probably still be there today. I was working toward getting my R.N. That's what I wanted. It was really rough on my wife because she had to work and do most of the supporting because they don't pay much at all, especially when you're trying to learn.

She did more for me than any person I ever knew. My wife is really a fantastic woman. I put her through some real hell. I started using heroin and then a lot of the love died. There was no competing with heroin. If there had been another woman or something she could have handled that, I think, maybe. At least she could have fought it. But with heroin there was no fighting because I was unreasonable. Not only when I would be going through stages of paranoia. I don't want you to think I was sick every day. There are times it gets worse, other times it gets really good and I'm fine. Most of the time I was, except I was still using heroin and when it comes to heroin there was no reasoning with me, no talking to me.

I would take the money we should use for the house and I would spend it on dope and that's all there was to it. She had nothing to say about it and it got pretty bad. I was surprised she stayed with me. I am truly surprised she put up with it. How, I'll never know. She doesn't mess around with drugs at all.

*You had a job, a good job, and a family life and money. What started you back on heroin?*

This is just a layman's idea but I do believe that at the time I was more afraid of success than anything else. All my life I had been told, "You're a failure." Their tendency was to lock you up and tell you, "You're such a louse you can't even be on the streets." This has been reinforced in prison. The prison environment reinforced it every single day. I'm 35608. You're not fit to have a name.

I believe I just wasn't coping with the idea that this is going to last. This can't last, you know. But as hard as it was, for several years there I stuck with it. I could never talk to my wife or anybody else about it because nobody would understand me trying to say that to them. I'd wake up in the middle of the night, sweating, thinking it can't last much longer. It would be easier just to drop it and split. They're waiting for me to do it. I might as well go on and do it.

*You thought someone was out to get you?*

I always felt in stress situations I was going to be the first one they'd pick out. I was going to fuck it up. Now I just never have that feeling. In that sense being in prison is more comfortable because here I don't have to try. Here the inmates accept me for what I am. I have probably an easier time in prison than most of the people do because I am accepted for what I am. In prison, even on death row, I have the respect of the other convicts because I know how to function in this lifestyle, which is really sick. It really is sick, but it's the way it is.

If I don't want to do something I don't do it. The hell with them. What are they going to do to me? Put me in the hole? They've already got me locked up in solitary confinement 24 hours a day. There's absolutely nothing they can do to me. So in that aspect it's easier.

But then when I think back about out there on the streets, the wife, the families, the people that I had met, the things I was able to get myself involved in I miss it real bad every single day. And that hurts. You take a man's freedom away from him, it doesn't sound like much, but you're really taking away the only thing in life that makes life worth living.

This is it for us. We're doing life and I don't think there's anybody down here who wants to give up life. There's nobody down here who can make plans either. I mean we're just here day after day after day. As far as revenge is concerned, if that's society's idea of capital punishment, they'd get a lot more revenge out of keeping a man in prison for life. And I mean life. I'm not talking about seven-year parole possibility, I'm talking about life. That's the most revenge you can get on a person.

The actual execution? The only part that's bad is the waiting. You're waiting for it every day. There's three individuals down here who have had dates set. Got down to the last two or three days. They've ordered their last meal, been allowed to call their parents to say good-bye to them and then were told, "No, you're not going to die now. Later."

This happens to people you know and care about, who live

next door to you. And you know they have to do that over and over. That's the hard part. Facing the gas chamber itself is not that difficult.

*You said yesterday that you're going to die in prison and that it may very well be in the gas chamber. You said people on death row can't plan their lives. What is the worth of your life? What is the value you put on it?*

Zilch. Zero. I don't think from one day to the next here. Wednesdays you're allowed to go to the store. If you have a little money you can maybe get an ice cream or something. Tuesdays and Thursdays I'm allowed to spend 45 minutes to an hour in a little cage where I get a little sunshine. Saturdays this time of year I can watch a football game. That is my plan.

I can hardly write a letter home. It takes me maybe three days to compose one letter because today is no different than Wednesday was four years ago for me on death row. We have no way of planning anything because we don't know what's going to happen. We may go to the gas chamber, we may not. We may go back to court, we may not. We don't know. And if they say, "O.K. for sure you're going to the gas chamber," it would be the same. You don't plan any kind of life. You exist and you wait and you wait and you think about it every day. Not your own death, but the death of the other people.

# Doug McCray

Shortly after the *Furman v. Georgia* U.S. Supreme Court decision in 1972, which found the existing death penalty laws to be arbitrarily applied and which eventually led to some 500 people being taken off the nation's death rows, Judge William Lamar Rose of Ft. Myers, Florida called a press conference. Judges, of course, don't usually express themselves directly through the media but this was different. The Supreme Court decision had piqued Judge Rose so that he felt compelled to make his views known in an unusual way. He took the small knot of reporters outside the courthouse and, decked out in a ten-gallon hat, proceeded to throw a handmade noose over the limb of a large oak tree. He had made his point.

On October 14, 1973 Margaret Mears, a sixty-eight-year-old white woman living in Ft. Myers, was raped, beaten and murdered in her home. After some initial hesitation the police arrested James "Doug" McCray, a local high school basketball star who had gone on to San Diego State University in California for the murder. Primarily on the evidence of testimony given by Otis Walker, an ex-convict who has since recanted, McCray was found guilty. After a sentencing trial the jury in the case recommended McCray be given a life sentence. The sitting judge in the case, William Lamar Rose, rejected this recommendation and sentenced McCray to death in the state's electric chair. Judge Rose made his point a second time.

At the time of this writing fully a third of the people on Florida's death row are there because the judges in their cases overruled the jury's recommendation for a life sentence. The reasons for rejecting a jury's recommendation are varied and sometimes not explained but in the McCray case Judge Rose was explicit. A death penalty was necessary, he said, to "set an example." After his retirement several years later Judge Rose told an interviewer that he felt at the time there would be little likelihood that the sentence would be carried out. John Spenkelink's execution in Florida's electric chair in May 1979 has greatly increased that likelihood.

Doug McCray's unusual sentencing is not the only quirk in his case. After his initial conviction, a new lawyer filed an appeal with the Florida Supreme Court. Oral arguments were heard on that appeal in 1975 and again in 1977, but as yet the Court has not ruled. On top of this extraordinary delay McCray's motion for a new trial on the ground that Otis Walker recanted has been denied.

Doug McCray's one word for all this is "shucks." That antiquated expletive, associated more with a college student in the '20's who has missed his bootleg connection than with a man under sentence of death in the '70's, peppers his conversation. When Judge Rose told McCray that he had been convicted by a "jury of his peers," McCray yelled back, "Those weren't my peers. All of the jurors were white!" His anger at the court is no less these days but the oft-used "shucks" softens it somewhat.

"Shucks" is a curious word. It means disappointment or disgust but when it is used the edge is taken off those feelings. It is the perfect word for Doug McCray to use. His death sentence has brought him and his family waves of disappointment, yet the dejection that attends such disappointment does not follow McCray everywhere. As we began our interview at the Florida State Prison in Starke, just down the hall from where his friend John Spenkelink was executed several months before, McCray was asked by a prison official to sign a release for the interview. "You want a big x or a little x?" he asked. Then, with three years of college to his credit, he turned the paper to show me his slanting signature.

"Ghetto hieroglyphics!" he grinned.

Doug McCray has a lively, quick intelligence, expressed a bit pedantically at times, and an engaging sense of humor. He is aware of these qualities and was concerned at the end of our interview that his manner not mask the seriousness with which he views his plight. His unconscionably long time on death row has been one that, simply by its longevity if nothing else, must grind and corrode the spirit. He has been able to survive that time with wit and grace. To meet him is to think that death row must engender this. It doesn't. My experience has shown me that everything about a death sentence willows the senses and the spirit. Doug McCray is alive and unbowed but he is also frightened, angry, and disillusioned.

> I HAD BEEN in jail for almost three and a half months before I knew that I could receive the death penalty. When my public defender came he said, "Well, Doug, what I'm going to try to do is keep you off death row." And I said, "Death row. They don't have that anymore." So he says, "Yes they do. Florida was the first state." So I went into . . . it was like being in a state of phantasmagoria or something.
>
> I went to the trial in a daze. After the jury deliberated, I can't remember the length of time, they came back and found me guilty. Then they retired to give a recommendation on the sentence. They took fifteen minutes to recommend mercy unanimously. But the trial judge said that he would have to think about the case and I was taken back to the county jail. A month later he sentenced me to die.

*How were you arrested?*

My Mom and I were eating breakfast and we were discussing the crime and, shucks, you know, we said to ourselves that we didn't think anybody could do such a thing. Apparently the guy who committed the offense had on a cast. At the time I did not have a cast but I had an ace bandage wrapped around my arm. So I was taken to the police department and questioned.

They detained me down there for about six hours and finally I became belligerent. I told them that if they didn't have any fingerprints or eyewitnesses or something like that, they had to let me go. So finally they let me go.

Three weeks later they had a guy in the county jail. He supposedly told the police officers that he saw me in the area of the crime covered with blood and everything. But since that time he has recanted his testimony and he has stated that police officers took him to the crime site and told him what to say and everything.

*And that's what you're basing your appeal on?*

Right, right. But I pled not guilty from the start. Even though they obtained a guilty verdict the evidence was just not there. Of course the doctor stated that they found presence of spermatazoa. The spermatazoa did not match my blood type. They also removed pubic hair from around the woman's vagina that also did not match. If I'm the sole person that committed this offense then all of the evidence should point toward me. But it does not. I attribute my conviction to the fact that I was given an all white jury.

*What kind of evidence did the state present then?*

Strictly circumstantial. They had this guy who stated that he saw me in the area of the crime and that I was covered with blood. And he said that I confessed the crime to him the following morning.

And so now I wait to die with all those questions there. And the only way that could be settled is for me to be given a new trial. But apparently the courts are not going to give me one because I haven't received a decision from the Florida Supreme Court yet. They've taken almost five years. I had oral arguments for a new trial in January '75 and they've yet to rule.

*Your case has moved nowhere from January 1975 to August 1979?*

It hasn't moved an inch. Nothing. Most attorneys I've talked to about it say that it is very unusual. They're just skipping over my case to get into others. They're ruling on cases now of guys who have been here a year. I had oral arguments shortly after Spenkelink. I was number ten when I came to death row. My appeal process should be way ahead. I should be in Federal Court someplace. But they would not rule on it. It's sitting right there.

*Do you think they are going to execute you?*
Honestly?

*Yes.*
I think so. I have tried to think otherwise, but take the South into consideration. Spenkelink was my best friend. If they could execute him for a crime as questionable as that where a crime happened behind close doors then, shucks, when they take my case, murder, rape, a young black charged with raping a white woman, shucks, you know my chances of survival are slim. Very slim. I just can't understand why, if they are so sure of my guilt, they won't just go and rule on it so all these doubts and questions can be answered. But they fail to do it.

*What did you feel like when you first got the death sentence? Were you aware of what was happening?*
No I was not. I was taken back to the county jail and I still didn't believe it. During those first couple of years I would pace up and down in my cell. I was writing everybody trying to get answers as to what was going on. Shucks, I recall writing my brother once and asking him, "Is this me in here?" you know, "I mean sentenced to die?" Shucks, I mean there were so many questions and I never got any answers. And I still don't have those answers.

I just can't understand the sentence of death, being sentenced to death. Shucks, I'm walking around all the time asking myself whatever happened to this great, to this once proud country, this great industrial maker. Our country is being defiled, ridiculed, spat on and everything because we're executing human beings.

I'm confronted with headaches, pains, and all the time I just can't understand it. Sometimes I say to myself that death could be, death has to be better than this. The victims were not placed in a cell and kept for years and then finally told that they would die on such and such a date. Now I don't mind dying but I don't want a time and place set for my departure.

*What did you feel like when John Spenkelink was executed?*

Oh I felt as if the entire country had failed John Spenkelink. The entire country had failed a warm, loving human being who cared for others. Society out there does not realize that they could have prevented John's execution. John wanted to live. He just couldn't understand it all. I would talk to John, sometimes all night long. He just could not understand why they were going through all of these motions just to have him executed.

And I sit back there and I watch the guys and I say to myself, "Now how could they sentence this guy to death, or this guy." You take Arthur Goode back there. Society and even a great number of prisoners here think that he is the worst human being alive and are wishing he would be executed. But shucks, the guy is a human being! And that in itself makes him special. He's a product of God. He's one of God's children. We are all God's children. So how can man say he should die?

My next-door cellmate is black, 24 and illiterate. I do all his reading and writing. Anyway the guy received a letter from a concerned citizen. The writer called him a human being. The guy made me read that particular sentence over and over and over. The thought of someone calling him a human being made all the difference.

The guys back there, they're poor, shucks, a great number are illiterate, they're black. We're the outcasts, the unwanted of society.

*Did you ever think about that before you came here?*

I felt those same emotions but I was not involved. I remember when I was younger I would read in the paper about a guy being executed. The only thing I could say was, poor guy. But being here has made me acutely aware of a great many things that I actually took for granted out there, one being human life. That is the most special thing that anyone can possess. And only God can take that.

When I was younger, in the second or third grade, Mom said I would go around the house, telling her that I would become President of the United States. After I became older and I began to see the attitude of society as far as me being black, of course the idea of me becoming President was so far-fetched that I'd say, "A black President? Never!"

Death row is simply psychological brutality. You question your dignity, self-worth and intelligence. A reporter asked me how long I had been on death row. When I responded by saying 28 years she thought I'd lost my senses. From my vantage point, such as it is, it's easy to see how black people are born with death sentences.

*What was your childhood like?*
I was born in Sacramento, California April 3, 1951, and my family migrated south when I was fifteen. I finished high school in Fort Myers. I attended junior college in Fort Myers, at Edison Community College, for two years and then I went into the service. After the Army I attended San Diego State University for one year. I came back down South to visit the family because I hadn't seen them in about three years and, uh, I'm here.

*Did you go to Vietnam?*
No, I went to Germany. I'm epileptic and so I would imagine that was a big factor in me not going to the war itself.

*How did you get into the Army if you were an epileptic?*
The army accepts epileptics. I had been an epileptic my entire life. For a period of four or five years there were absolutely no seizures. And so at the time I was in the service there were no seizures or anything. But during basic training, for some strange reason I started having seizures. They wanted to discharge me at the time but I would not sign the discharge papers.

*Why?*
Well you see at the time I went into the service I wanted to be in. When I left junior college I had offers to attend other universities on a basketball scholarship but I discovered I had been going to school my entire life so I wanted something new. I really went into the service for a twenty year hitch. After being in there for a year and sixteen days I was given a medical discharge.

*For the epilepsy?*
Right. From Fort Riley Kansas.

*Were you happy as a kid?*
Yes, I was well loved. I was well loved as a child. Shucks, I can recall my childhood as being happy. Of course we were always poor. I can recall when we had to eat grits on wax paper because we didn't have any plates. But we were always happy. Shucks, you know, there's something special about being poor and black. I can lie on my bunk back there and I can think of the times when we wouldn't have anything to eat at home so we would

raid the orange grove, you know. We would haul back these sacks of oranges. And so we would eat oranges for the week.

Being poor, there is a cohesiveness that's unthought of in the affluent neighborhoods.

My Mom and Dad always instilled in me the importance of getting a good education. Even though there were a great number of us—I have four brothers and three sisters—they would stress education more than anything. I could be lying in bed, you know, starving almost, and then my Mom she would come in there and say, "Doug, did you study tonight?" you know. And I always said to myself, "What's wrong with this woman? I am starving! And she's telling me something about a book."

I was pretty bright as a child. When I became older I knew that my family would never be able to send me to college. So I turned to athletics.

My mother is the strongest person and she only has an eighth grade education. But she has been a source of strength to all of us. I've always wanted her to be proud of me, you know. I remember when I enrolled in junior college. Shucks, she took me around to every one of her friends and she said, "Doug is starting college on Monday." I mean she was so proud. I was the first and only one to go. That made her so proud.

And then when I was arrested I felt more than anything I somewhat let her down. Not as far as my guilt or innocence but from the fact that I was charged with such a horrendous offense. And I told her after I got the death sentence that regardless of whether I'm executed or not I don't want her to ever feel that she failed me. I think she pretty well understood.

*Do you see your family at all?*
No.

*How come? They're not in Fort Myers anymore?*
My Dad is in Fort Myers.

*Your mother and father are divorced?*
No they are legally separated. For about six years now.

*And your mother is out in California?*
Yeah right. Dad is not what you would call rich. He doesn't have the funds to come up. But whenever he can save up enough money he will come up and see me. My Mom she works seven days a week as a maid trying to keep money to my

attorney. After I was convicted they got all the family together and retained another lawyer. A great number of friends joined in also.

Let's see. I've been on death row five years and four months. I think I've had three or four visits all together from my family. You just can't come down from California to Florida whenever you're ready.

*Let me ask you about your epilepsy. Do you have seizures now?*

Yes. I'm on medication. I take 400 milligrams of dilantin in the morning and I take 100 milligrams of phenobarbital at night. But I still have seizures, especially during the summer because the hot weather makes me more susceptible to seizures. I was told by the doctor that I could possibly be bringing my own seizures on because of the worrying, stress and anxiety. I said, "Well, look man, I got a death sentence, you know! So how can I not worry?!"

An incident happened a few years back. We went to the exercise yard. When you go to the exercise yard the room to the electric chair is out there. They were cleaning the room to the electric chair. The water fountain is ten yards from the room that houses the chair. At the time they had the blinds down, and so on my way back I looked back and saw the electric chair. I went into a seizure, it frightened me that much.

I don't think I ever thought about the death penalty that much until I saw the chair itself. And that has to be the most horrible thing I have ever seen. I get up in the morning, go to bed at night and I'm thinking of it. My cell overlooks the room they have the electric chair in. They have the light on in there. And as hard as I try not to look over there it seems as if something draws me to it. It's really like death hangs over us back there like a cloud.

I'm so sick of hearing, "I wonder who is going to be next." After Spenkelink's execution it has been extremely hard. I have had a great number of seizures from that. I've complained to counselors, requesting to move from that side. Even when the ambulance came in, you know, we were all looking out the windows seeing them lower Spenkelink's body into the ambulance and everything. Now this has to have an effect on us back there and I think that they are deliberately doing this. Whenever a warrant is signed I go back to the morning of Spenkelink's death. It comes right back and I go into an attack. I get extremely sick.

*Have you had a severe attack?*

Back in '75 I had an attack and I broke my collar bone. It was the next morning when they were passing out breakfast that they found me on the floor. On another occasion last year, I don't even remember what happened but I remember trying to yell out. The doctor tells me that when they were finally able to get me down to the clinic they rushed me over to "The Rock" across the street over there and they didn't have any beds so they had to rush me to Lake Butler, which is ten miles away. He said I was almost dead. He said that I couldn't breathe. I had swallowed my tongue. I was unconscious for three days. When I got up, of course, my tongue was raw. I had bitten it.

Now that is another strike against me. Shucks, not only am I a black man with a sentence of death but when you have a medical problem such as mine it's even more destructive. Society still has this outdated idea that epileptics are somehow possessed by the devil, or evil spirits or whatever. Heck, Socrates, Aristotle, Julius Caesar and also Beethoven had epilepsy. Add Doug McCray to that list and you've got quite a crew!

*Were you ever married?*

Yes I was married to a beautiful young lady from Jacksonville, Florida named Myra Starks. We were only married for a couple of years. We had a beautiful child, a son, Donny. We had conflicting ideas about what we both wanted out of life which led to a separation and ultimately our divorce.

*Does she come to see you?*

No. She's in Sacramento.

*Do you ever see your son?*

No. I haven't seen him since I've been here. I write to him. I write to both of them. And he is such a beautiful child. He is very gifted. He goes to a school for mentally gifted kids. They're considering putting him in another program. He's in third grade but he works on a seventh grade level. Shucks, he writes as if he's fourteen. I can talk to him about Mr. Carter, the SALT treaty or anything and he's up on it. Shucks, I cry a lot because of him. I can watch a ball game on TV or something, and I think of the San Francisco Giants out there where I would probably have him up in the stands with me. You know we'd be going to the ball games or I'd be taking him camping or, shucks, I love jogging. I can just see us doing all those things together. And shucks, I'm missing the best days of his life. I just feel alienated. I'm only thankful that his mother has instilled in him that he has a father. A great number of women say, "Hey, he's locked away with the death sentence," and that's it.

*Can you see any situation where capital punishment might be needed?*

There are a great number of cases back there that, whenever I think of them it almost makes me vomit. I guess society is confronted with a problem that a person does something so bad that they just have to kill him. Which is a comment on society. One of man's most ugly and primitive emotions is vengeance. Capital punishment is only a short-sighted manifestation of society's frantic search for a panacea for all these problems with crime. I'm sure that Governor Graham doesn't actually think that capital punishment is a deterrent to crime.

What really gets me is that society treats capital punishment as if it's an abstract social concept. Shucks, I thought that Spenkelink's execution would bring an awareness to society out there, but it seems like the popularity of the death penalty escalated with his death. Iniquity always stirs more popular excitement than virtue.

# Rebecca Machetti

On August 31, 1974 Ronald Akins and his bride of twenty days, Juanita, were murdered in Macon, Georgia. It was Akins' second marriage. Three people were arrested for the murders: Rebecca Machetti, Akins' first wife who had herself remarried only a month before the murders, Tony Machetti, her new husband, and John Maree, a friend and sometimes house guest of the Machettis. Maree and Tony Machetti were charged with the actual murder and Rebecca was charged with murder by virtue of her role as a conspirator. Maree admitted his role in the slayings, testified against the other two and was given two concurrent life sentences. Tony Machetti denied involvement, was convicted and sentenced to the electric chair. Rebecca Machetti likewise denied any knowledge of the crime and was convicted and given two consecutive death sentences. She then became the only woman on death row in Georgia and the only person there for a conspiracy role in a murder. The state has never claimed she was at the scene of the crime.

Before meeting her I was told that Rebecca Machetti was an "experience." From the moment we met in the glass-walled cafeteria that serves as the visiting room for the Georgia Women's Correctional Institution in Hardwick, Georgia, I was not disappointed. A woman of medium height and brown hair she glided across the empty room to where I was sitting, wearing a big, warm smile, over-sized sunglasses, a bright yellow jumpsuit and an orange chiffon scarf. She soon described herself as "overweight and talkative." The former is an exaggeration, the latter an understatement.

Rebecca Machetti is an exemplar of the noble southern tradition of story telling. Educated and articulate, she spins out a greatly detailed narrative in a soft southern accent. Her inflection combines the best of preaching, backyard gossip, Clarence Darrow and the movie stars of the forties. I exercised my vocal chords little in our long conversation.

While we talked groups of woman inmates passed by the cafeteria. Hardly a group would pass that she would not wave to someone and interrupt what she was saying to pass on a story about whoever it was she waved to. At other points she held court there in the room. Guards came to say hello, to ask questions of her, to seek advice about some detail. She knew many of them well and would tick off a list of questions about the guards' families, problems and pleasures. She is clearly an institution within the institution. Locked in her room nearly twenty-four hours a day, a threat to no one, she is nonetheless a counselor to many.

But Rebecca Machetti's life, I soon found out, has been a difficult one, a complex web of highs and lows laden with manifold contradiction. I could not then nor can I now straighten out all those details that seem out of place. I'm not sure she can either. Her life seems to be two movies running at the same time; one is a romantic comedy, the other a hard-bitten, real-life tragedy. Machetti stars in both, adoring her role in the first, confused and hurt by her role in the second. Her verve throughout is unflagging.

Rebecca Machetti is a forty-one-year old mother of three daughters. She went to college after her children were born, earned a degree in nursing and worked in Miami as a nurse before her arrest, her first ever, in 1974. She grew up in Athens, Georgia and was an only child until the age of fifteen when a brother was born. She describes her childhood as happy and filled with love. Tragedy struck, however, when in her senior year in high school her father, deranged by a brain tumor that had gone undiagnosed, killed her brother and then committed suicide.

After the tragedy Rebecca quickly married Ronald Akins, thinking mistakenly that doing so would ease her mother's difficult financial situation. She and Akins soon had three children. The marriage lasted sixteen years but the divorce in 1973 came after years of separation and serious problems. Rebecca says that Akins treated her very poorly, had homosexual encounters, and drank excessively. After her divorce she moved from Macon, where she and Akins lived, to Miami. There she began work as a nurse for three doctors in an office.

Her life in Miami is a bit shadowy. The district attorney in Macon at her trial tried to paint her as the queen of the Mafia but she says she was far from that. She spent time at the horse track and said she did well. She gave parties and says that she was a mother figure to many people in the area. She seems to have a fascination for things Italian, which was perhaps part of her attraction to Machetti.

For someone as maternal as Machetti perhaps her biggest disappointment in life has been her children. She feels that she has failed them. Grown now, they do not write or visit her. In talking about her daughters Rebecca halted her narrative and cried softly. Though we talked about some possible reasons for her failure with her daughters, her relationship with them remains a mystery to me and perhaps to her too.

She lives an energetic life on death row. With the full support of her mother and stepfather she has waged a legal effort to have her conviction overturned. Her stepbrother, who is now seventeen, is like a son and his achievements give her great pleasure. She writes many people and conducts what she calls a "prison ministry" sending sermons and devotional materials to a number of other prisons around the country. A convert to Catholicism, she has blended her new faith with the Methodism of her youth to form what must be something of a unique ministry.

Women on death row are unusual. At this writing there are seven of them—less than one percent of the death row population. Four of those seven were convicted with husbands or boyfriends. People on death row for conspiracy to murder are also rare. Although a completely accurate tally is not at hand, a rough survey indicates that the percentage of death row inmates convicted of conspiracy is as small as that of women on death row.

Rebecca Machetti may be statistically unique but the oddities of her case have not exempted her from the normal procedures of a death sentence. Three times now some aspect of her case has gone all the way to the Supreme Court and three times her appeals have been denied a hearing. Shortly after our interview a date was set for her execution and a stay was granted by the United States District Court. Because Georgia's death penalty statute was held constitutional by the Supreme Court in 1976 the likelihood Rebecca Machetti will die in the electric chair at Reidsville remains.

That, of course, bothers her. But her attitude toward her own death sentence is typically complex. No, she says, she does not want to die. Yet, she continues, if her death in the electric chair, the death of an "innocent person," could stop the death penalty and save others now facing capital punishment, she would be consoled.

MY BIRTH CERTIFICATE reads Clarke County but I was born before I ever got there. That's where the doctor found me and Mama so that's where I'm listed as bieng born. I was born in a brass bed in a bedroom that we're not sure who owned the house of and when we got to Clarke County the doctor who came had known my mother all her life and he said, "Well, we'll register her birth here."

I am one-eighth Cherokee Indian, I'm one-eighth Scottish, I'm one-eighth Italian, I'm three-eighths English and I'm one-quarter or two-eighths Irish. The Scotch has enabled me, when I make money, to save. The Irish has given me some wit. The Italian has given me, I think, a hint of beauty and the English has given me a sense of knowing who I am, a sort of aristocratic feeling.

I came from very humble origins. We never owned a car until I was probably seventeen years old. I grew up in a home that had a wood stove that you fed with coal or wood. For a long time clothes were washed in a wash pot in the back yard. I have slopped pigs, I have tended cows, I have run from roosters. My grandmother's one of thirteen children. They all got married and had ten or twelve so the family is enormous. I was raised in Athens.

I was an only child for thirteen and one-half years. My brother lived for three and a half years and then he died and I was all alone. My stepsister was born after I had married and had children. She died at birth. Then my stepbrother, who's seventeen now, came along in 1962. He's really like my son.

I would go grocery shopping with my parents on Saturday morning. Once we brought the groceries home we put them up and we'd go to town and we'd have dinner. Every Saturday. Two hot dogs at a place called Patrick's and a cherry smash and then we walked. We'd go down to the newsstand. Comics were a dime and my father would give me a dollar and he'd say, "You may buy ten." Sometimes, if my mother wasn't around, I'd hide my comic books in a sack. Maybe she was off doing women's business. I preferred to be with my daddy and I didn't go and look at dresses and all, even though she made me wear them. So she would say, "Where have you been?" and I would say, "Daddy took me to Patrick's and got my hot dogs and cherry smash and now I want to go to the newsstand." I never told my parents a lie in my life. But if she didn't come out and ask me . . .

We didn't have a car. We walked everywhere we went. So we would go home again and put all our parcels up from shopping and we'd hit the theaters. We had three: the Palace, the Strand, I never went there, and the Georgian theater. I could get in for twelve cents, my parents for a quarter. Now, you mind you, I'm six or seven years old, maybe a little older than that. We'd go to one theater and I'd get my popcorn and my Coca-Cola and I'd watch that movie. Then we'd go directly to another one. I grew up on John Wayne and Rory Calhoun and Marlene Dietrich and Claudette Colbert and Bette Davis and Broderick Crawford. Daddy would come out and he says, "Well, ya'll gonna see one more movie?" By that time it was dark at night. He says, "Do ya'll want to walk down to the fish place and have some fish?" Most of the time we opted for fish because my eyes was tired.

Sunday morning it's up, go to church, then across town and out in the country to grandmother's where there's fried chicken and fresh cured ham and corn on the cob and sliced tomatoes and all kinds of preserves and jellies and big old thick buttermilk biscuits. Then that afternoon it's visiting with all the relatives. And then if I can get over and nudge Daddy I say, "You know that movie we didn't see last night?" He said, "This is Sunday." I said "I won't tell." So on the way home we'd stop off in town and see the third movie.

I come from an old family. While we may not have all that
much, we were respected. I wore the little gloves and the little
Mary Jane shoes that were shined with margarine to make them
look pretty. They seemed to forget that they also attracted flies!

I came from two environments. My godfather in the church
was the reigning judge in North Georgia, Judge Thomas, long
since dead, God rest his soul. My godmother was his sister who
had traveled all over Europe. I was reading probably at age four
because the judge had a huge library. I think I knew about
Africa even before I learned how to spell it. And I was shown
by my godfather, you know, this is the route Napoleon took and
this is the Himalayas and all this. Of course I learned about
Blackstone, heard about the English Parliament, English law.
He had a dictionary which had its own stand on the floor. And so
by the time I got to first grade I just sat there and smiled and
talked a lot. I made good grades every report card from first
grade on up. There would be this nice blue slip in there on my
scholastic abilities and then at the bottom we would have
"conduct." My teachers would write "talkative," "talks too
much," "excessive talker."

*Hhmm. I can't understand that!*

I think I was a child that was allowed to be herself and to grow
within limitations. I was more or less allowed to explore the
things that my mind was desirous of knowing. My parents made
every opportunity available to me whether it was through a book,
or whether it was through an actual experience. When I was
taken to the shore, mollusks and shells were explained to me,
the tide and the effects of the moon and this sort of thing. When
they'd take me to the mountains, the clouds we looked down on
were explained to me.

I decided I would be a nurse and so I brought home sick dogs.
Had to keep them on the back porch and in order to keep them
there, to keep them from running away no matter how sick they
were, I managed to tie 'em down. When they got healed I still
wouldn't let them go home. I had sick dogs, cats, chickens,
rabbits. Finally one day this black lady down the road brought a
sick goat up there and that was the epitome of my surgical
expertise. I said, "What's wrong with the goat?" and she said,
"Well, I don't know if anything's wrong with it. He's just acting
kind of weird. He ate a chenille bedspread." I had sense enough
to know I couldn't slice the goat open and pull the bedspread out
so I decided I would get the goat to regurgitate the bedspread. I
had this great dream that I would wash the bedspread and go
flying down the road and tell her. To make a long story short the

goat almost died because I gave him so many laxatives that between vomiting and everything else that he was doing, well, the poor goat he'd almost wasted away. Never did get the bedspread out of him.

In high school I was in the drama club, the Civil Air Patrol airplane spotters club, which gave me a pair of wings and absolutely no knowledge of anything aeronautical. I was on the basketball team and I sang in the choir and I was on the debating team and anything and everything, you know. I stayed real active. My parents raised me in the church. Although I'm Catholic now, I was christened a Methodist.

I was a virgin when I married. I never made out in the relationships I had in high school from 9th grade. I wasn't allowed to date until I was close to 15. Then I had to go in a cab and come back in a cab. If the guy came in a car, he had to park it. My mama and daddy wouldn't let me ride in it. And if I walked anywhere in the neighborhood I had to call when I got there and call when I got ready to leave, even on a date, mind you now. I could go to church with him, I didn't have to call. If I went to his parents' house I didn't have to call. But if I went anywhere else I had to call. But anyway I was just always a good buddy to guys.

There was never any locker room talk about me, you know. It was, "Is Becky gonna help you get through your calculus exam? Becky sew that number back on your jacket?" Cause I more or less mothered a lot of people there that's mothers just didn't seem to do too much for them. I was the same age they were. I'd take on the responsibility of washing football jackets and jerseys and doing things for all my friends.

Just because I've had some bad deals in my life doesn't sour me on the fact that men and women both have mutual feelings. You want to be loved, you want to feel like people like you. When you smile you want it returned. I understand when you've got a pimple on your face and you've got a heavy date that night or, you know, I understand these things. Men are human beings and I don't treat them as little boys. I see them as somebody just like me. They hurt.

The father I had and adored committed suicide when I was a senior in high school. The three and a half year old brother that I had? My father took my brother's life. Later on we were to find out that my father had a massive brain tumor and was at the point of desperation and certainly illogical thinking. That happened in November of 1955.

I was a senior in high school. I only lacked I think maybe finishing up 12th grade English and possibly Latin. That was about it and I could graduate. So I started getting into class at

1:00 and I went to work. Because my father killed himself, there was a clause in the insurance policy that said no insurance whatsoever. But we got $500. It cost, with buying vaults and the coffin and all the funeral expenses in the neighborhood of $4000 to bury my little brother and my father. The insurance company gave us a check for $500. My mother went to the bank and on the family's good name she borrowed the rest of the money. We owned no home, no furniture, we owned no car, we owned no property. It was strictly a huge loan on the basis of knowing what a person's integrity was and the fact that they were exactly what they projected themselves to be.

I had already been informed that I had a scholarship to the University of Georgia. I also had one to a couple of other colleges. I had done extremely well on the SAT's and I thought the world was my oyster. Then in November it tumbled down. I went and talked to the principal at the school who took me into his heart, so to speak, and said, "Anything that we can do for you we will make available." And I said, "Well, there's no way I can go off to college now because my mother has got to go off to work. We're just going to have to fumble by." I didn't realize, I knew nothing about Social Security or the fact that there would have been a Social Security check coming for me plus one for her for taking care of me.

So I got it in my head that I would be a burden to my mother and I ran away and got married the Saturday after I graduated from high school. I did not love him but I thought I was giving my mother an escape route. We both could say, "Well, she was in love and it happened." I would thereby reduce the financial burden I was upon her, never realizing that when she would report to Social Security that I, at age 17, was married, all payments to her would stop and she would really hit financial rock bottom.

But anyway, though the marriage was wrong, by the time that I got sense enough and thought about an anullment or possibly a divorce I realized I would be the first person in my family to do something like that. I got to thinking about all I had forfeited. Fall was coming and everybody I had graduated with was going off to William and Mary and Stanford and the University of Georgia, Georgia Tech, Harvard, Yale, Cornell, Tulane and there I was . . . By the time I got to do some serious thinking, I was pregnant. So, raised in a family where you married for better or worse, you made your bed, you sleep in it, this sort of thing, irrational, illogical teachings of the Old South put into its young women, I slept in the bed that I had made.

I had one child and then when she was ten and a half months

old I had another. Time walked by and the man that I had married turned out to be not supportive of me. My parents wound up supporting me. By this time Mama had remarried. The stepfather I have now I call my father. I very seldom ever think about the other father I had those years in my childhood.

After severe problems in my marriage I decided that somewhere, some way I would get myself out of that mess. It took me another ten years. I was determined that I was going to get a B.S. degree in nursing so I worked as an aide, and I worked as an attendant. I just finally got up enough education so I could go and get a license for practical nursing. I carried fifteen hours in college every quarter. By this time I had given birth to a third child. I have three daughters.

My husband was still in the house. He was bad but poverty and being out in the world on my own trying to raise three children sounded worse. So I was willing to endure that hell to avoid a worse hell until I could stand on my own and say, "I am a woman, I can do this and walk away from him." So that's what I did.

I wasn't content with cakes and pies and rolls and biscuits and filling the freezer and the shelves with canned goods. I sewed and did upholstery. I got tired of that once I knew I had accomplished it. I wanted to go on to something else. I taught in the Baptist church. I was Vice President of the PTA. I raised quarter horses and showed them. The money I got I raised my children on. My husband, in almost four years, never gave me a dime except to make the house payments and pay the utilities.

I finally moved to Miami with my children, got divorced and I married again on July 27, 1974. I married this man who was vice-president of an insurance company from New Jersey. And approximately four weeks after this marriage took place these murders occurred. My new husband was not at home with me. I saw him on Friday morning. I didn't see him again until Sunday. He left me and I raised hell. I really did. I told him, "Hey, house guests are coming down and we're supposed to be newlyweds." I love the man or I think I do. And he says, "There are some things I got to do. I'm going to do them and you can just go to hell." So he left that morning, going to the office. I never saw him again till Sunday. Sunday afternoon late I got word to call my mother and I did. I found out these people had died and one of them I didn't even know, I hadn't heard of, because my first husband had apparently married again, had been married about 20 days.

I just couldn't believe it. Then the next day I started suspecting I was under some sort of suspicion. About six weeks later I came home from work one night with my cap still on my head, my nursing uniform on and seven men came out of my house. Two of 'ems got sawed-off shot guns and the rest of 'ems got .357 magnums, all of them pulled. They tell me I went to Georgia and killed two people. I ain't killed nobody and I set about trying to tell them where I'm at. I go to jail and I waived extradition and went to Georgia thinking that I would wind back up in Florida again when they all found out the truth. I've never seen Florida again.

I can't tell you anything about Machetti and that's the truth. I cannot tell you anything because he has always denied his involvement. I got the words of John Maree. He was on the scene and he described it. In the weeks between the day of the murders and my arrest he would come to me and tell me "Yes, I killed them, I killed them."

He never once claimed I paid him a dime, so he couldn't be a killer for hire. He claimed I forced him to, quote, unquote. I used to kiddingly say I wished I could get a patent on this supersonic gun that's got a barrel six hundred miles long that you can be in Miami and pull it on somebody in Macon and make 'em do something. After a while I even quit saying that.

The trial was a farce as far as I'm concerned. The DA got up and said that my motive was revenge and an insurance policy in the neighborhood of $20,000. The children were the beneficiaries on the insurance policy to be split three ways and to go into trust for them until age eighteen or when they would enter college. There would never have been any money whatsoever for my hands to have touched. I read someplace a while back in the *Star* or *Enquirer* that I hired a killer to kill two people for $100,000. One of the staff members here read it and she said, "Have you seen it?" and I said, "Yeah, I got a copy of it in the mail." She said, "Rebecca, when are these people going to start telling the truth about you?" "Gee," I said, "I don't know. Maybe never. Maybe nobody will ever come to know the truth."

My family decided that with the little money we had we would get a family lawyer from Athens. Right before my second brother was born things got super good for my mother and stepfather. It seemed almost like they were being rewarded for all those years of abstaining from greed and being content with their lot. Then along came all this and they sold cemetery plots, cash in insurance policies, they use my brother's college fund, they take a big loan on the house, they sell one of the cars, they wipe out everything.

I had a 78 year old attorney. We had known him 30 years, I guess. He had not tried a case under the new death penalty. It had been a good 12 or 14 years since he had even tried a criminal case. He had become somewhat of a property-type estate lawyer. He was hard of hearing. He didn't want me making a scene. I might have really made a scene. I was very naive. I was placed in a situation where I could be manipulated. I was scared slap out of my mind with this talking about this electric chair.

I was sentenced to die at seven minutes after one in the morning. I had been upstairs in the jail. We didn't know the jury's going to come back. The judge didn't dismiss them but my parents thought he would. They went back with my children and my brother, who at the time was close to being thirteen. They went back to the Hilton where they had taken rooms, which is in walking distance of the courthouse there. So when I was sentenced to die I didn't have anybody in the courtroom that's on my side.

I felt like I was sitting out there. I knew they were talking about me but it just didn't seem real. It seemed like I was back over in the corner and able to look at myself and look at other people talking about me.

The lawyer goes to shaking and doing this number like he's got St. Vitus Dance and I turn around and put my arms around his waist and I say, "It's gonna be all right." And then the judge sentences me to die and tells me how many may be present at my execution, any members of my family, the clergy and any members of the legal team that helped fight for me and anybody else that I might want and tells me how these invitations are sent out. And then he asked me do I have anything to say. And I'm still standing there holding up my shaking lawyer and I looked up at the judge and I said, "Thank you, your Honor, thank you very much." And I turned around and left and helped my lawyer to the door where his secretary took him.

They took me back upstairs and when I got upstairs, the dam, just like Boulder Dam, broke. God, I cried until four or five o'clock in the morning. I never sobbed. That lady held me. She was about six foot tall, a huge black lady. She just pulled me on her lap and held me while I cried and cried and cried. And finally I calmed down and she let me call Florida to tell a friend of mine who hadn't been able to make it to the trial, to tell my bosses, three Jewish doctors I worked for, to tell my bosses that I had been sentenced to die and please pray for me.

And then I went back and woke everybody else up in the cell block when I came to the door. I didn't deliberately mean to wake them up. And they were all there saying, "Machetti, what happened? Have you been down there all night?" I said, "No. I've been up there on Miss McEroy's lap, crying." And they said, "What did the bastards do?" And I said, "They sentenced me to die," and I said, "The man tells me I will, that I will die."

I had no reservations or thoughts about the death penalty whatsoever until it came home to me they could take the life of an innocent person. I'm not even too hot on taking the life of a guilty person.

We have one woman here who killed her common law husband, cut out his heart, placed it by the side of him and went and made a cup of coffee, drank that, cut off his sexual organ, put it into his mouth, went to town, did some shopping and came back and finished cutting him up in little pieces. We have her serving life. We have a woman who's gone home from the institution now after serving approximately four and a half years. She cooked her baby and served it on the table to her family. And here I am. I was in North Miami Beach, in my home, when these two killings came down in Georgia and it is stated, documented fact, irrefutable, that I have not taken a life. And I am here on the testimony of one man. He's serving life concurrently and I'm serving death consecutively. If the juice don't come the first time it'll come the second. So I look around and I see the variation and the discrepancy and the fact that it is strictly the whim of the District Attorney. You put a dart board up there and sling a dart at it. This one will die and this one won't. If I don't make it out of here I'd like to leave some precious memories for some people to see that possibly the system is wrong. The system needs some cleaning up.

Somebody, somewhere along the line has got to care. Somebody has got to give and not really care about the consequences. I do not want to be a Martin Luther King or a Joan of Arc or any of the saints but I have thought that perhaps somebody innocent has got to go to the electric chair to end this forever. I don't want to do it but if it would end this atrocity in twentieth-century, democratic America, then perhaps that desire I have to save mankind might be the epitome of serving. I don't have any suicidal tendencies or anything like that but, Doug, something has got to end this nightmare.

So I just sit back and I smile and I do my needlepoint and I run my prison ministry and I watch a little TV and I study law and I study the Bible and I communicate with people and I see people right and left in here turn their lives over to God, because of God, not me, but God using me to say, "You think you've got problems? I mean, you know, your husband's running around or your child's got to have braces or you were in a wreck or you gained thirty-five pounds? Hey, Babe, you know, at least you've got your feet in those shoes. I've got no feet, you know!" God has allowed me to feel like I'm not wasting my time.

I run a prison ministry and have run it for about four years. I write to at least one penitentiary in every state of the Union and some abroad. I do sermons now for 17 institutions across the country once a month; two youth development centers, five state institutions, ten federal institutions. The only thing I ask for in this ministry is I say, "Hey, I don't care where you have been. I care where you are going."

*Do you think you'll be executed?*

The way I look at it Florida paved the way to kill black people by making the first sacrifice a white person. Georgia may well bend over just a little further to show their democratic way of rendering justice. I will be the first liberated woman to go to the electric chair and they'll say, "Well, not only now are we showin' you we're not being prejudiced, not only are we going to kill a white but we're going to kill a white woman."

But I don't think Georgia is ready to send a woman to the electric chair in this day and age with all the civil activists about. I think they've got a lot of explaining to John Q. Public and to the judiciary and to the newspapers and so forth why they see fit to kill someone who was not on the scene, did not take a life, when they have women in this institution who have killed up to five people.

I may spend a lot of time in here until the truth comes out. I think I will go out of here this way: very dramatically with some landmark decision being set down or some overwhelming judiciary decision by some judge somewhere which says, "Set that woman free!" It'll be just like Paul and Silas staying in jail in the Catacombs of Rome and the door was all of a sudden burst open and the jailer's there and he's quivering and shaking and they walk out.

But that may be a fantasy. I believe there's enough people out there who doubt my guilt and enough people that know me for who I am that it's going to be a big splash. It ought to be. It was a big splash when I came here. It ought to be a big one when I go out.

I like me today, I think, more than I did five years ago. And I know more love today than I've ever known in my life and I grew up in a very loving environment. No, Doug, I'm not afraid to, not afraid to die. I don't want to die. I'm not too hot on being in the bosom of Abraham. But I'm accountable for my actions in here and I'm not ashamed to read the book of life on me. Love is the name of the game. Friendship is right up under it and I got both of those and I intend to keep them.

# Jimmy Lee Gray

Any crime for which the death penalty is given is detestable, but there are degrees of repulsion. The first-degree murder and attendant molestation of a child makes most of us sick with sadness and hate. Even in prison, the violator of an unknowing innocent earns loathing; the child molester behind bars has reason to fear assault and can expect to spend his time in cold, withering isolation.

I am not different from others in this respect. When I met Jimmy Lee Gray on death row in Mississippi I knew he was there for the rape and murder of Deressa Scales, a three-year old girl in Pascagoula, Mississippi. That created a prejudice in me that remains now and will not go away. But my prejudice has not brought me to the point of saying that the crime of child rape and murder should be considered a capital crime even if no others are. After spending hours with Jimmy Lee Gray I could never say that he should be put to death, even for that most horrible crime.

Jimmy's own mother feels differently. After the 1977 conviction of her son, Mrs. Verna Smith, now living in California, wrote the Mississippi Supreme Court and Mississippi Governor Cliff Finch asking them not to stay Jimmy's execution. She now lobbies for capital punishment.

Jimmy Lee Gray lived with both his mother and father as he grew but at different times. They were separated when he was eight and he and his two brothers would shift back and forth between his mother's house in California and his father's in Arizona. He speaks of his parents in cold, biting, clinical terms; he feels that they provided him with nothing and taught him anger and destructive repression of that anger. In his senior year in high school that repression could not hold back a tide of anger that he vented on his girlfriend, whom he killed in an argument.

Gray spent seven years at the Arizona State Prison for the murder. For the first several years he used drugs heavily (drug traffic in most big state prisons is quite heavy). In the last few years of his term he began a second life. He learned computer programming and worked for several state agencies with his programming skills.

Those skills carried him through his release from prison and for several years after. But he lost one job because emotional problems interfered with his work and he felt pursued by nightmarish feelings he could not control. He moved from California to Pascagoula for a computer job and in a short time he was arrested for the murder of Deressa Scales.

Death row in Mississippi is in a squat concrete building on a road of work camps in Parchman State Prison on the flat, bottom land of the central Mississippi delta. On the hot summer day I arrived there the small, nearly windowless structure, surrounded by guard towers and a single chain link fence looked and felt like a place of punishment. Big fans inside the front door failed to move air into the rows of cells but succeeded in covering every nook and cranny with a cloud of droning noise. I went into a little visiting room that had some mattresses on the floor and some screens, that were just thin horizontal bars, to separate the prisoner from the visitor. It was hot so I opened a door that opened on the yard. A flock of mosquitoes outside the visiting room buzzed a counterpoint to the omnipresent hum of the fans.

Almost oblivious to these distractions Jimmy Lee Gray sat down opposite me across the visiting table. A thin, short man of thirty-two, he looks much younger. He was not expecting my visit and my cameras. He was unshaven and apologized for not getting spruced up. It took me a while to tune my ear to his speech and volume. He speaks through tight lips and does so very softly. He is shy and has trouble looking up as he talks. But his embarrassment did not last throughout our conversation. At times he would make a point forcefully and directly. His anger came out at times, not in raised volume or tone of voice but in the choice of words he used to describe those things that upset him. He seemed aware of his emotional problems and informed about them by a combination of fundamentalist Christianity and books he reads on Christian psychology. He describes his emotional disturbance in very broad terms but he seems convinced that they accurately depict the causes of his troubles.

Gray could not talk about the two murders he has been convicted of. Our conversation changed immediately when I asked about the crimes. In the case of the murder of Deressa Scales he was visibly troubled by having to think about it and could only speak about the death in the most passive terms. He spoke of how the prosecution had dropped a charge of unnatural intercourse but how just having that charge prejudiced the jury. He did not deny his involvement in the crime but in talking about the murder he could not place himself in it. Clearly he had no plan to try to convince me he was innocent. I could see why a judge or jury might not think him insane. He could talk quite clearly about the charges against him. But a combination of guilt, fear and remorse along with severe emotional problems that I don't have the expertise to name, have made the memory of the crime much too painful to be brought out.

Most prisoners walk around the word "arrest" as if it were an open manhole. The thought of their own arrest is so unpleasant that just the word itself scares up a flock of unwanted feelings. Jimmy Lee Gray is different in this regard. As you will see, there is a certain amount of solace for him in the memory of his own arrest. Something he couldn't control was controlled for him.

I WAS BORN in Whittier California and I spent half of my life in California and then the other half in Arizona. It wasn't just half in California first and half in Arizona. It was back and forth.

I was born September 25, 1948. In '56 we went out to Arizona and stayed there until Mom and Dad were divorced in the early sixties. After that I did a lot of moving around.

I had two brothers. At first we were all staying with my Dad and then they went to live with my mother. Then there was a little division out there. So they went to stay with my grandmother. My older brother had a lot of trouble.

*Where did you come in the family? Were you the youngest?*
No. I was in the middle.

*What did your father do?*
He didn't do anything. That's why I kept leaving. It seemed to me that my mother didn't do anything either.

My whole childhood and my teenage years and everything, it was miserable. There was a lot of inner turmoil. I see that now but I couldn't see it then. Even after I physically became an adult I still didn't understand what was happening. I was very lonely and I caught myself searching for love. I wanted to find love somewhere and I didn't have any peace at all.

*How did your parents deal with that?*
Well I don't know because my parents, they understood very little about love either. Everything we did was motivated by emotions and things like that. So there was very little control over any of our lives. My older brother was under a lot of emotional stress most of the time. I was under a great deal of emotional stress because my environment wasn't one of love.

I looked around me and I seen a lot of anger and a lot of bitterness and a lot of hatred, a lot of envy and jealousy and fear and all these things. Somebody said children live what they learn and that's true. I grew up not being able to trust anyone and being afraid of everyone.

I seen all these things happen around me and, now, inside, way down inside I knew that these things were wrong but still I saw them going on around me and I said, "Well, maybe they're not wrong. Maybe I'm wrong." And so it was easy for me to justify punching my brother in the nose when he tried to hurt me or something like that. My older brother and I fought a lot.

I got my share of abuse with a big, thick, leather belt. My parents would go through the day and they'd collect up all these anxieties and frustrations and what-have-you. I didn't want to do nothing wrong if my brother had done something wrong just before me cause they would build up a little bit, you know. I don't just get punished for doing that wrong. I get punished just because they've got a lot of anger and bitterness and all these things built up inside 'em. And so I'm really getting punished more than I ought for this stuff.

But I'm an introvert and the worst kind of introvert, too. Reality is painful and so I just withdraw from it into little fantasies. They were just kinda like daydreams, really. But it was a better life, no complications, you know.

I wanted to do something to help people. I always felt that way. I wanted to change the world and make it a better world to live in. So I was always doing something like that; writing songs cause I used to play the guitar. Anything that would give people positive emotions instead of some negative ones.

*How did your schooling go?*

Well I was in my twelfth year, my second twelfth year at Parker High School in Arizona when I was arrested for murder out there. I was nineteen at the time.

It was like down through the years we build up all these anxieties and frustrations. This was in December of '67. I went to Los Angeles to spend Christmas with my family. I got there and everybody was fighting and arguing and it was just miserable. Christmas to me should have been a time for love, you know. And I left, I left early and I went back to Parker and my high school teacher took me to Wyoming with him to spend Christmas with his family.

That was the most enjoyable Christmas I ever had. And on the way back I was thinking how I really hate to go back to this. And we passed by the Utah State Prison. I looked at it. I didn't say nothing to my friend. But I looked over at him. He was looking at me, you know. And I think he knew something was wrong, too.

Well, we wasn't back from Wyoming but a week and I murdered my girl friend. We had gotten into an argument and she had kind of a wild temper and she hit me and I just blew up. I couldn't . . . for several . . . I didn't even know that . . . in a way I justified doing that, you know. I thought it was right to do that. And in another way I didn't think I did it at all. It took me a whole year for the realization to finally sink in.

I don't doubt that I loved the girl. I think I really did. But the emotional problems at the time and everything at the time it just had my head so messed up that I couldn't think.

I went to Arizona State Prison for seven years. The first three years I wasted pretty much. I got into drugs and stuff like that.

*In the prison?*

Yeah. I had never messed with it too much, well about maybe two or three times I had smoked some grass, but I didn't really care about drugs or drinking or sex, either, really. Those are the things that I did just to feel accepted in social groups because I didn't feel like a part of group. I've always had a lack of self-esteem, really.

I did some acid in prison and, uh, too much, I think, and smoked a lot of grass and shot up a lot of junk and stuff. But my last four years in prison I seemed to get myself together a little bit. I knew I had a problem, a very severe emotional problem.

Well I learned how to program computers. I graduated at the top of my class. During those four years I programmed for the State of Arizona. They had two computer systems. I programmed those. I did some work for the Department of Corrections and for the Department of Health.

When I got out of prison I got me a job with a company called Comtax Corporation in El Segundo, California. They compute income tax returns. After I'd been out for a while those problems, little problems, started to develop and my emotional problems started to get worse. I noticed that I couldn't any longer concentrate on my work. It takes a lot of logic when you're writing computer programs. And so that's what happened. When I get emotional, my logic just falls all apart.

*Did you start using drugs again?*

No. I smoked a little marijuana every now and then, maybe on a social occasion, but I never cared anything about it, about drugs or anything. I always wanted to know where I was and what I was doing. I was really afraid of them, you know.

*How did you get from El Segundo to Mississippi?*

Well I lost my job out there in California. I couldn't tell my boss what was the problem. He asked me. He gave me a good chance to save my job but I just couldn't tell him what was wrong with me. He asked me if I needed money and I said, "No, I don't need any money."

I was working on the Colorado individual returns and he called me in one day and, after he had taken a look at the program and it wasn't working at all he said, "We're going to have to let you go." In a way I felt kinda bad. I was a little scared. But I was glad. I was glad to be out from under that pressure cause it was constantly bothering me. I'd go to work in the morning worrying about whether he was going to fire me or whether he'd say something to me.

*Was there anywhere you could go to get help at this point? Did you try to see a psychiatrist or something like that?*
No. I didn't try to do that. When you're under pressure like that you don't think about things like that. You're looking for other ways of escaping. It's like Christianity. There are so many people running around out there with problems and they're looking for all these little escape routes. But there isn't but one and that's Jesus Christ, right? And he's right there for everyone to see. But nobody sees him.

*You didn't see him at the time, I take it.*
No. I even went to church one time with my uncle but that was cause I wanted to get together with him and play a little music. I wanted to show off my new guitar. But I didn't know nothing about Jesus.

And there was too many other little ways of trying to avoid reality. Lots of times what I'd do I'd get in my car and I'd drive and drive for hours and hours, you know. And I'm not going anywhere I'm just driving. It's a wonder I didn't get arrested out in California before I come to Mississippi. I think I would have been a lot better off out there.

*What happened in Mississippi?*
I moved to Pascagoula. While I was in California I got a job with a company called Programming Methods, based in New York. They sent me to Pascagoula. I was working for the Ingalls Ship Yard and their little claims project. I helped write statistics they needed to sue the Navy.

That was interesting for a little while but as I say problems evolved. I think if no problems had come up I would have created problems. I just got under a lot of pressure, I guess. And I started doing things that I shouldn't have been doing.

I was arrested for . . . well I'll tell you what they say I did. They say that I kidnapped and raped and murdered a three year old girl. They had an indictment one time that charged me with unnatural intercourse. I know these people know that that never happened. We got 'em to drop that but we can't get 'em to just leave that subject alone at all. See they need that. It's prejudiced the jury cause when the jury hears something like that, you know, it just makes them sick. They say "Well, this guy . . . this guy is . . . let's give him that death penalty."

*Were you aware of what was happening?*
I don't know. I wasn't . . . I'm not really, well . . . I'm aware that this child left the apartment complex with me. Now that is kidnapping, O.K. At the time it wasn't kidnapping to me. I didn't think it was kidnapping. And I certainly didn't intend for that child not to come back, you know. I wasn't really aware of how . . . I wasn't aware of what happened out in Arizona too much, you know.

*Did you know her family?*
I'd just seen 'em a few times. And I talked to her father one time. He had an alligator in the trunk of his car or something. It just bit his thumb. I stopped by to check it out but he wasn't too friendly for some reason. I had never done anything to him but, I don't know, he just didn't . . .

*Did you see them during the trial?*
Yeah. He had pretty good control over himself. Right after the death of this child his wife had one that was stillborn and then a miscarriage and then they got a divorce. She was very bitter, very angry. I can't really blame her. She sent word up to the jail that somebody ought to kill this fellow. She actually tried to get somebody in the jail to do something to hurt me.

*How did you feel about the girl?*
I felt bad. I still feel bad about it. It's still a really painful thing for me. When I do think about it, you know, I realize that I'm responsible because if I hadn't taken her away she wouldn't have died, see. And when I think about that that hurts me a lot. Because I've always liked children and this one, she reminded me a whole lot of my niece. My niece was only two and I hadn't seen my niece in a long time. But it just hurts a lot.

*How did your family respond to it?*
Well my mother responded by writing a letter to the Supreme Court and asking them not to stay my execution. My older brother, he's in a convalescent hospital out in Los Angeles. He's nearly a vegetable. My youngest brother, he doesn't write to me anymore. My Dad, when I was arrested in Arizona it was reported to me that he had said "I don't want to get involved." So that pretty much ended that relationship.

But as I was growing up I never knew I had a mother and father. And just all these little things that happened during the years just confirmed what I felt inside. I just didn't have a mother and father, nobody that I could turn to or talk to. I wanted to feel close to my father but he just never gave me nothing to feel close to him about.

*How did it affect you when your mother wrote and said she wanted you executed?*

I didn't hear about it for a while but when I did hear about it I suppose I . . . well I was a little amused, in a sense. And I was embarrassed, and angry and bitter. There's a lot of bitterness in me right now.

*You were amused? That's kind of a strange emotion for that kind of thing.*

I thought it was in a way. I don't think it's funny anymore because there is something seriously wrong with her. The family on her side has a history of mental illness and disorders and stuff like that. In the words of my grandmother, "They were a bunch of lunatics." I think she's disturbed mentally and emotionally. She tried to kill herself three or four times.

*If your sentence was commuted do you think you should be let out?*

I think I should get some help before they do anything. I asked them for help in Arizona. And they gave me a psychological test. The results were that I had a 95% chance of marked disturbance and a 3% probability of moderate disturbance and a 1% probability of mild disturbance in a given situation. So that leaves 1% of no disturbance at all. If there's a problem I'm going to be 95% disturbed about it, you know. And that's true. I see little problems as great big ones and they're really difficult for me to overcome. But I think that that can be fixed. I'm sure of that. And I've done quite a bit just by reading God's word. But there is still something deep down inside that I've got to . . . It's just going to take time to work it out. But I believe it is possible for me to have some control over my life instead of being shoved around by these emotions all the time.

*Have you ever felt that you had to pay for your crime?*

I always believed that if somebody did something wrong they ought to pay for it. I always believed that way and I'm not going to change now. I never have been in favor of the death penalty because I think that there are a lot of people that can be helped in this world if somebody would just stop and do something with them. I don't think they should put anyone to death.

*Do you feel you are going to be executed? Do you think about the gas chamber?*

Naw I just get up in the morning. I usually wake up with a headache because I got a problem with my neck. But I don't think about the gas chamber. When they were working on it, fixing it up I thought about it but it was just a passing thought. When one of the other fellows' execution date comes up and there's a scheduled execution I think about it more and it makes me nervous. I don't want to see any of the guys back there going to the gas chamber.

There were times when I actually felt it would be better if I were executed. I just couldn't go on. But that was like when I was first arrested. I don't know. I don't think I'm going to be executed. I just don't believe that to keep going. I think that it's in God's hands and I really believe that. I think that whatever he wants that's what's going to happen. But I don't think I'll be executed. I think I can do too much good for this world. Even from prison I can do good. I can write, maybe help somebody. Maybe somebody will have similar problems and they'll read a book that I've written or something. Maybe it'll help them understand themselves.

*You talked about getting involved with Christianity. People on the outside look at that sometimes as a way for someone on death row to try to save their neck.*

Jailhouse religion. Well that's true. People, you know, they need the love. First place they need to believe there is something more after this life. But there are some who are just kind of devious and they say, "Well I'm going to read this Bible and learn all about it and I'm going to get me a minister's license while I'm here in prison." And people out there are going to see this and they figure it's going to get him off.

God controls all of these things. I'm not going anywhere unless God wants me to be there because it's His will that's being accomplished in this world today. He's even in all of the evil that's happening. God's not evil but he will allow something to happen to bring some good out of it.

I was arrested in June '76 because God wanted to get me in a place where I couldn't move and get away from him anymore. When I was out there in the world there was too many places I could go, too many things I could do, you know, to escape from reality. See me being in jail I can't move around. I can't go anywhere.

*Do you suppose you're going to have to spend the rest of your life in prison?*

I don't know. I really don't know. I want to make the best of my life wherever I am. I'm trying to mature mentally and emotionally now. That was the problem I had when I was growing up. I didn't have any help. Nobody encouraged me to say anything. My parents said children should be seen and not heard. I never learned how to express myself. I just held these things inside. Even if I do spend the rest of my life in jail I can do some good. I think I can help.

*Do you think you should be in a hospital?*

Yeah I'd be better off in a hospital. Just to get some help and not just to get out of paying for anything I might have done. I don't know about this Mississippi State Hospital. When I went down there it looked like the place was a mess. And it didn't look to me like they were doing anything but prescribing medicine for people, maybe zap 'em with some electricity every now and then to kind of shock'em out of something.

I been down there twice. The first time I refused to sign a committment paper because I thought they were going to try to get me all drugged up or something and I'd be a zombie when I left. They didn't even bother examining me. They want to know how smart I am. They want to know if I know I'm charged with a capital crime and that I could get a death penalty. As long as they know that then they figured they can take me to court. They don't want to know what my state of mind was at the time of the alleged crime or anything like that.

I've been looking at myself from a psychological point of view. I've got a Christian psychology book back there that I'm reading and it's helping me quite a bit. I think I got a pretty good understanding of myself. Now what I need to do is fix the problem. I built the machine and I crash a lot because I'm dealing with positive ideals on one side and negative on the other. All my fears and everything on this side. All my desires to become a better man on this side. They're just warring against each other. When I try to make those ideals a reality in a negative society like this prison I'm already shot down before I get the ideas out there.

Nobody's following their conscience any more. Everybody's being their own God. That's the way I did so many years. My emotions were pushing me around. My conscience would tell me don't do something and I didn't understand what the conscience was all about. My conscience would say, "Don't do this," but to me my conscience was saying, "You're afraid." Now I looked at that as being fear and fear to me was something to overcome. I grew up thinking a man was supposed to be big, hard-working, strong and afraid of nothing. So I was trying to overcome all these fears and all the time I'm doing stuff that I shouldn't be doing. It was a challenge to me and I had to overcome that fear. I understand it now.

# Phil Brasfield

Exactly a year to the day after Phil Brasfield arrived on Texas' death row, we sat down to talk. Death row in Texas is at Ellis Unit, a maximum security prison, one of a cluster of prisons outside of Huntsville. We met in a large brick-walled visiting room next to the row on a weekday when the room was nearly empty. We sat at a long table that was divided down the middle by a brick wall underneath and mesh reinforced glass above. Brasfield wore a white, prison-issue jumpsuit and his hair, like that of all the men on Texas' death row, was close-cropped. He placed pipe tobacco, a pipe and a pipe tool on the table, smiled slightly as we nodded an awkward introduction, and folded his hands in front of him, ready for the interview. Then he remembered something and turned around the glasses case protruding from his jumpsuit pocket. On the other side was a white button with red lettering that read, "Why do we kill people who kill people to show that killing people is wrong?"

Phil Brasfield was convicted of the murder of Johnny Turner Jr., a six-year old black boy who was kidnapped, molested and killed on October 25, 1977 in Lubbock, Texas. Brasfield, a frame carpenter and drug and alcohol abuse counselor who lived in nearby Slaton, has maintained his complete innocence of the crime throughout and is basing his appeal of the conviction on that claim. Because of the nature of that appeal he and his lawyer agreed that we would not talk about the specifics of his case.

He has always been something of an outsider. Raised by middle-class parents in Slaton, he attended parochial school, was an altar boy, participated in Boy Scouts, won music awards and did fairly well in school. But in Slaton, a wind-whipped collection of houses, his family's acceptance of blacks and his father's recurrent bouts with alcoholism, did not put him in the mainstream.

As he reached his twenties he saw more and more differences between himself and the people of Slaton. He too had a drinking problem and was nearly killed because of it. Once, when driving under the influence, he lingered too long on a railroad track and was hit by a train. He survived but soon gave up drinking. He had a rebellious streak that the local police identified and he spent several short stays in the local jail for minor violations. He joined the Navy but was released shortly after he had injured his foot in a rifle accident and had protested the Vietnam War in his uniform. He further separated himself from his contemporaries in Slaton when he joined and worked for the War Resisters League.

He found himself when he began doing drug and alcohol abuse counseling, which he learned and practiced in Veteran's Administration hospitals in Texas and Colorado. His first marriage ended in divorce and he kept custody of his two daughters. He met and married a fellow counselor and eventually operated a group of six detoxification centers in Colorado. When funding for those centers ran out he and his family moved back to Slaton to live in a trailer he owned there and to paint his parents' house. Shortly after he moved back Brasfield was arrested for Johnny Turner's murder.

He does not feel any more an insider on death row than he did in Slaton. A quiet, almost shy man he views death row with the detached eye of a social scientist. He applies the language of self-help counselling (phrases like "grief work") to his own feelings and to the feelings of others on the row. During this, his first time in prison, he is more concerned about the deprivations brought on by prison life than he is about the possibility of his own execution.

And he is apprehensive. He is clearly out of his environment, somewhat fragile and sensitive in a milieu of regimentation, constant noise, embittering boredom and outright physical threat. He is a man of words in an atmosphere of active, non-verbal intimidation.

Phil Brasfield may not feel like one of the death row population, he may have distance and detachment others on death row don't have, but the possibility he may be put to death by injection is just as great with him as it is with all 135 other death row inmates in Texas. He is an insider until the day the courts agree with his side of the story.

I CAME HERE a year ago today. After receiving the death penalty in March of '78 I stayed in solitary confinement in the county jail for almost two months before I came down. Before the trial it was something like three months in solitary. From the night the police came to my house till right now it has been 561 days. They say you don't count the days but I can't help it.

If you can call going to death row pleasant, for me it was pleasant. One of the deputies that brought me in I had known for about a year. He is a gentleman before he is a lawman. That is very good. He treated me with respect all the way along. The other deputy was a guy I had gone to AA meetings with so we knew each other too. It was a very calm drive down. They handcuffed me in transit but when we stopped I was un-handcuffed. I kept the handcuffs in my pocket and when we got back in the car I snapped them on myself.

It rained on the way down and the guy driving played western music. Willie Nelson sang "Blue Eyes Crying in the Rain" over and over again. The closer we got the closer they watched me.

We went by Diagnostics where they dropped me off. They became nervous and put on their little official masks and let me out with my toothbrush and drove away without saying goodbye. I guess it was hard for them to say goodbye too.

I was starting to enjoy myself on the drive down, looking at the trees and the flowers which I hadn't seen in quite a while. The change was rather drastic at Diagnostics. There were 60 or 70 guys who just came in off the bus, the Chain they call it, and they were lined up without their clothes on, waiting to go through some sort of inspection.

I got priority treatment. I got my clothes off, stripped down, got my beard and hair cut, took a shower, went up and was fingerprinted, got mug shots, came back down and got into white clothes similar to these and within ten minutes I was here at Ellis Unit. Diagnostics put me in the back of a van. That's the first time that anybody ever looked at me with evil intent while they were holding a gun. One guy was driving the van and the other guy sitting with a shotgun pointed at me. I guess that is supposed to let you know where you are and where you are headed.

We arrived out here and they un-handcuffed me and took the shackles off my legs and gave me some very good advice, "Keep your nose clean, boy, and mind all the rules and you won't have any trouble." I followed that advice and haven't had any trouble at all here.

*Do you remember anything about your thoughts a year ago?*

I was frightened, totally frightened of prison. I'd heard the common stories that you hear about things in Texas prisons and Southern prisons in general. They don't have that good of a reputation. I talked to people all my life who had been in prison who told me about the corporal punishment that went on and the gang rapes and, you know, all the horror stories. Plus I didn't know how I was going to react to a situation where I was locked up with killers, guys that I had read about in the newspapers. It took me about two months to get to the point where I would trust them. I would go out and do exercises and for two months, literally, I stayed by myself and watched them, checked them out. And they were checking me out. They were wondering what was wrong with me—I didn't talk or anything.

I've kept a journal ever since I came here. I was re-reading it last night and there are a lot of scary things in it. After those two months in solitary I was really frightened. I didn't talk to anybody except for the guys at the shower where there was conversation back and forth. I was that way for two months. That period was the worst.

*That was worse than the solitary confinement in the county jail?*

Well, I don't know. In solitary it was probably the first time that I have ever been able to get in touch with myself. I did a lot of grief work because my father died while I was there. I had taken him down to the hospital in Temple a week before I was arrested. They arrested me and he came home too soon and had that oxygen off. He came to see me in the jail and I knew when I saw him, and I think he did too, that that was the last time we were going to talk. And he went home and died two days later.

So I was dealing with that grief plus dealing with a sense of non-reality that seemed to surround me, by being convicted. I had to get down and do a lot of grief work, not only for my father but for myself. And I worked out a lot of things, using the tools of the trade, counselling, using them on me. I rejected a lot of it and also accepted a lot of it. And it was then that I started to read the Bible also, which has helped. I don't buy all of it but I accept a lot of it. The basic philosophy of loving yourself and other people I grabbed ahold of.

Like I said I had heard all the horror stories. People in the county jail went out of their way, because of the case, to come by and tell me all those stories, the things that were going to happen to me, the threats of castration, rape, all of these things. And having never been here before I didn't know any better.

I got down here and just had to sit back and wait and see, not risk any of myself in any way. The guys on either side of me gave me cigarettes and I said to myself, "Oh, my God, they are trying to get close to me," and you know what that means in prison. If you have nothing in prison and some nice guy comes and gives you something, whatever he gives you, cigarettes, coffee, whatever, if he wants to collect later and you don't have it then you are wide open to sexual favors and things like that. And I don't want anything like that so I would not accept anything from anybody.

There was one guy who told me in Spanish one night, "I'm not trying to make a move on you. You are going to have to decide what to do." He's been in prison for 18 years. The man on the other side of me asked me if I was a Christian. I said I didn't know, I would like to think I am sometimes. He said he was a Christian. And it went from two people to four and four to six and now I know about 30 people on death row. None of them real close. Something keeps us from being involved very deeply in each other. I suppose it's the threat of not knowing whether that guy will be here.

*I wouldn't expect that. I would think that if you knew someone was not going to be here long, was going to be executed, you would want to get to know him better. Why isn't that so?*
Because of the risk. If you get close to anybody you have to risk your feelings. You risk either rejection or acceptance. And the men that I have known, they don't risk that much. The majority of them have been hurt very badly before coming here, by their own situations, by being in trouble at an early age, reform school, which was a prison before. And there is a terrible lack of trust among individuals. They don't trust the guards, they don't trust each other. Whether or not they trust themselves, I don't know. They are not willing to risk anything except, well—not feelings. They have no trust.

I took a risk just last week. A man's wife died in Houston and he wasn't allowed to go to the funeral. He found out in recreation. All of us were joking and laughing at the time and he found out and everybody left. He was left literally by himself. But I couldn't leave him. I got up and went over and made some coffee, ran hot water and made instant coffee and gave him a cup of coffee and told him not to keep it in. I don't know. I told him he would have to deal with it eventually and everybody would understand if he let it out. And he started letting it out, you know, shedding some tears, that sort of thing. I don't care that it was me but after the group saw one man do it, the rest of them started coming around and saying something or just patting him on the shoulder. I've seen men imitate positive things like that.

I found out then that the guys will follow the leader. There is no individuality as far as group behavior and I think that death row inmates, here at least, are more easy in that regard than the general prison population. Out there it is supposedly dog eat dog whereas here we are like so many victims of a large shipwreck and stick together almost all the time.

*As far as prison security is concerned you definitely are treated differently. Why is that?*
I have no idea. Because for the past year that I have been here with death row men I have seen no difference, basically, from the guys in the street. Circumstances are definitely different. But unless it is in extreme circumstances of stress, they don't act any differently from anybody else. We are people here. I say we but I think "they." I still have that problem, differentiating between me and they.

*It's hard to consider yourself one of the death row population?*
For me, yes.

*How long are you locked down during the day?*
Except for maybe ten minutes for a shower, twenty-three hours and fifty minutes.

*So you are locked down all day then. What is your routine?*
When I first got here the time just stretched out so long during the day that in two or three weeks I was about to climb the walls. I've been in jail a couple of times before but never for months and months at a time. So at first I didn't have any sort of routine. But then I bought a typewriter and now I have a routine. It goes something like this: I get up at six in the morning. I read for an hour, I've got some books for inspiration. I'll eat breakfast and read a couple of chapters of a book and then I will spend a couple of hours answering letters before the TVs come on. And usually by ten or ten-thirty I just read or write.

*Do the TVs bother you?*
Oh, yes. We have these large wall-mounted TVs outside the cells. There are ten on each side and those suckers are on too long for me. The volumes are turned up and there are a lot of people playing the radios and maybe one guy talking to another guy from the first tier to the third tier. The noise is fantastic. At first I couldn't deal with the noise. But since that time I put cotton in my ears and that helps. But I read something like a book a day, book and a half.

In the afternoon that's all I do and then at night the mail comes in. I'll go through the mail and write some letters. I write some for the prison newsletter here and I've been working on that.

*How did you come to write so much? Did you write when you were on the outside?*
I wrote some short stories. From the time I was sixteen years old I wanted to write. And after I wrote a couple of short stories I just never had the time, or never took the time until now. And I have an excess of time now.

*So your day is basically reading and writing. Does that contrast with some of the other men on the floor?*
I believe so. Every day there is somebody who asks me to write something—to write their lawyers for them, to write a letter to their mother or a girlfriend or wife, so I do that. They give me the

basics of what they want to say and I will just rearrange their words and enlarge what they want to say. Many of the guys are stuck on the television which to me is not entertainment. It is a pacifier.

*Do you get any exercise at all?*
I exercise myself. I have a box that I sit on and I'm at my typewriter a lot, hunched over my typewriter. I have to get up and put everything away and do jumping jacks and push ups and sit ups, that sort of thing, just to keep in shape. Outside I play volleyball. We've been allowed out three times so far this year. The other days have been inside. There are just not enough guards here to watch us.

*So you spend a great deal of time in that cell. What is that like?*
It's six feet by nine. In one corner is a sink. Right next to that is the toilet. There are two wall mounted boxes and that's all. No writing tables or anything. I understand that on the other side there are small writing tables. I've never been on the other side.

Besides those things I have a fan, typewriter, books. They make you shave. No radios or anything. We have a small wall-mounted radio and you can get only three channels on it. One is a Western music station, one is a disco station and the other—I don't know what it is. I don't listen to it.

We have one sixty-watt bulb on the back of the cell. I'm lucky because I have a cover on mine so I can direct the light up or down. I can turn the light my way when I work at night. And we have florescent lighting in the hall outside the cell. But that's on our side. On the other side the cells don't have any lights at all inside them. So once the sun goes down those guys are literally in the dark except for the reflection of the florescent lights outside plus the TV glow.

*There are no lights in the cell?*
No. There is no electrical outlet in most of the cells either. So they run extension cords. A younger guy wanted me to come over and look into his case, which I try to do sometimes. But I won't go because I would lose my light. I didn't know that until recently when I was talking to him and he said there was no electricity in those cells.

*Why did they make one row of cells with light and one without? This prison was built in 1963.*
From what I understand that section at one time was used for administrative segregation. And, by the way, we still

have, I think, five cells above us where the men are still in administrative segregation.

*You said a while ago that you were frightened coming here. Do you think you were more frightened of prison than you were of the death sentence?*

The death sentence so far hasn't bothered me that much. I've seen other people die in different situations—old age, sickness, we've all got to do that. Whether it is mandated by law or whether it is from natural causes, there is no way of escaping it. So *per se* the death sentence didn't bother me. I think that mainly because I shouldn't be here and I feel very sure that I will get a reversal. So this hasn't really touched me very closely. If I got a date set and lost the appeal and had to deal with, well, next Thursday I'm going to die, it would probably bother the hell out of me. But so far I've only watched other people die here. There is one guy who is on his third hunger strike. It is not to protest the food. It is just because he doesn't want anybody to stick a needle in him. He is trying to take his own life rather than somebody else take his life.

Just like this button says, I can't figure it out. I can't figure out how capital punishment changes anything or makes anything better. A crime is committed and it is a tragic thing for many people, not only the victims and their immediate family and friends but also the perpetrators and their family and friends. It's like throwing a rock in a pool and the waves go out and long after the center of that pool is calm those waves are still going out.

Capital punishment doesn't change those waves. Violence begets violence. It is a shame that someone doesn't value a life and takes a life but it is so much worse, in my mind, for the state to devalue a man's life. If a man steals something you don't go out and steal something of his to show that stealing is wrong. It just doesn't make any sense.

I can't dwell on that death sentence. I know it is there. It is a threat to a certain extent but because there haven't been that many executions in so long and because of my feelings my case will be reversed it is not that much of a threat. I know one man pretty well that possibly will be executed, maybe this year. And he has dealt with the possibility for say four and a half or five years. He's done very well, I do think so. But I can see that it is gradually wearing him down. He is becoming more irritated, more withdrawn from the crowd, much less tolerant of people than he had been before. And I have seen that sort of reaction in so many people—it's like a terminal disease. They start cutting ties long before death comes. It's like withdrawing into themselves. And I guess that is just some sort of protective mechanism a person has to protect not only himself but the other people around him.

*What is the alternative to the death penalty?*

Certainly not life imprisonment because I can see no help for people by keeping them in prison for the rest of their lives. The other alternative that I can find in my own mind is a lot of years for sure but not empty years, because they can be empty. You do all this for years and years and you become bitter.

See I don't agree that rehabilitation doesn't work. I have seen in the helping profession too many times that an almost helpless person has been helped when people cared enough for him and showed him that they cared by being there, you know?

The news media doesn't attack the alcoholic or the addict or the mental patient quite so much as they used to, even five or ten years ago. There is more public understanding for those people. There should be more programs to enable them to get their lives into some sort of a more positive shape. However, the criminal, and that is a label I don't like, the person that is convicted of a crime, is immediately stigmatized, taken out of society, put into prison and there is literally forgotten, for all practical purposes. There is a strong minority out there, and I hope it grows, that is going to be more interested in the plight of the prisoner.

I've got some guilt behind me, I think. I wasn't that interested in what happened to people once they got to prison. I was like a lot of people in the street now. It didn't concern me until I experienced it or saw it.

This is something that has been on my mind ever since I got there. Nobody up here is fooling me, at least, or really each other, when they say that they don't care, about themselves or about each other. Every man has feelings about himself and about the guys around him. It is un-macho to express those feelings but if you watch people or are trained in behavior at all you can see it and pick up on it. The saddest thing I see is the way people pretend. Death row isn't full yet. There are four cells not full. There are musicians up there, artists, people with writing talent and I always feel sorry for them because they play a big part, I suppose, in wasting that potential that they've got.

Some of the men here never give of themselves. I'm afraid if they never do they will destroy themselves. That is something that is tragic. You listen to some of those histories, when they open up a little bit, and can tell that they were really messed over when they were younger—parents, society or whatever. All of us have to be responsible for our own actions. There must be some way to make men responsible in a positive way so that their entire lives will not be messed up from now on.

*You are married aren't you?*

Yes. Josie comes from a town that is probably less than 300 people. She's moved from West Texas to Houston to be closer to the prison. She's done well to adapt to the environment and living with me and going through this trial and moving to Houston. We've had many problems lately and I have tried to take the stance of being understanding and supportive to her. But it is hard for me because I don't have that much coming back in. I need the support too, you know. But we'll be getting that. I don't give up on people. We'll get it worked out. Jo and I had my two children from my first marriage. They are living in Dallas now with their mother, my ex-wife.

*Do you see your kids, have contact with them?*

Yes, they come down. They have been down three times in the last year and I get a letter every two or three weeks. Two girls. The oldest is seven and the youngest is five. My seven-year old just wrote her first letter to me herself.

*What has been the hardest part of the last year?*

Being away from my kids, not seeing their first years, and not seeing my father buried.

*They wouldn't let you go to his burial?*

No. They were good enough to take me down to the funeral home and let me go in through the back entrance and see him for about ten minutes. That is the last time that I touched the kids. They were there but I couldn't hold them because I was chained. So I couldn't hold them or hug them but they climbed on me and hugged me. That is the last time that my family was all together and I was with them, there with my father's body. I'm still not resolved to that fact.

The other hardest part is every time I see my wife, my mother, or anybody in the family. I don't know if it is my thing reflected in their face, or their own but I can see the pressure. I have adapted to it. It is unpleasant but I have adapted to it. At one time I couldn't take the pressure. Fear of the unknown, I guess. So when they come to visit there is always—well it is hard to see them go. It is hard to be as close as we are and not be able to touch them.

There is a lot of importance in physical touch. We are not

allowed conjugal visits so at least we should be allowed to sit and hold hands or embrace or kiss, you know. I have not been touched by another human, except to be searched for weapons since I came here. I have never touched another inmates hand. And you really get—well I sometimes just want a pat on the back. The touch of another human hand is important. For all of us. Deprivation of strokes.

*What does that do to you?*

Well, it is an emotional need that is not fulfilled. So, as in anything, I think, if it is not fulfilled, it sort of dies off, if you are not really careful. I express myself much better writing now than I do talking. So I share what we are talking about with Josie and she shares back with me through writing, on that ink and that paper. But that can't account in any way for what we feel, what we need.

It's involuntary celibacy—I don't know. You have to meet those needs in certain ways and the only way that we can on death row is masturbation. That is one of the cruel things about being here. There is a certain degree of inferiority that I have knowing that my wife has equal or more needs than I do and knowing that she has the option to find fulfillment in other people where I can't. It drives a wedge between us, whether spoken or not. I talked it over with a guy here and he said I had to get rid of my old lady because I couldn't stand that pressure. He said I had to just tell her that we were through.

I hope that never happens between Jo and me because I can see where it just might. There is a constant wondering, you know, and worrying about it. If I were out there and she were in here I would have to be honest and say I wouldn't be able to remain faithful. So I can't judge her if she chooses to tell me and I can't hold it against her. That is just a biological need. I know that probably she wouldn't do that if I were still out there.

I would give anything, second to holding my children, to be able to hold her, or be able to hug my mother when she comes here. She is sixty-four and there is no guarantee that she will be there when I get out. She is healthy and all that but there are just no guarantees.

*Does she get to visit you often?*

No. The tension and prices keep piling up and she is alone. She has to drive four-hundred miles plus to get here. Last year she made three trips all by herself. It is sort of a shame for her or you or anybody to have to drive all that way and just be able to stay a couple of hours.

*How has she taken your situation?*

I don't know how she has done it, stood up to the pressure and the heartaches that it has caused her. And it was compounded when my father died. She had to deal with that plus my being convicted sixty-one days after he died. She has become not religious but more faithful and she is starting to turn a lot of things over to a higher power. She goes to Alanon meetings because of my father's difficulty with drinking and plus my own difficulty. I was a boozer for a while, three or four years. I did that until I got run over by a train and survived. And she has stood up. She works and stays busy all the time.

*Where does your support come from?*

From friends of mine, my mother, my sister and wife. I get a lot of support from a doctor who was one of my teachers in Colorado. He's a psychologist up there and we write back and forth. And I read. Jesus, in his day and age, was sort of a revolutionary kind of guy. I get inspiration from that. And I also get it from myself. Sort of self-discipline. I haven't given up. It comes from the little three or four year old kid that I was a long time ago who couldn't breathe because he had asthma. But he wouldn't give up. I guess I've always been like that. I guess it's stubborn. I'm too damned stubborn to give up.

*What was it like actually being sentenced to death?*

When we went there and the foreman gave a slip of paper to the judge the judge looked surprised and looked down at the floor. Then he looked at the jury and read the sentence. When the man read my death sentence to me I saw my father sort of pull back. It was something like I watched on television so many times before, expecting dramatic news and getting that.

*How would you compare being given that sentence with being hit by a train?*

The train was quicker. The train was softer.

# Mike Moore

Mike Moore and Chuck Brueck were friends in the late summer of 1977. Mike, twenty-eight at the time, a Vietnam veteran, recently separated from his wife, was almost like a big brother to Chuck, who was eighteen. They partied together, dated together, drank and smoked dope together. Moore, an over-the-road truck driver, went around Memphis on a souped-up road bike and was known in many of the city hangouts as "Fudley."

In September of that year Mike Moore shot and killed Chuck Brueck near Memphis. On parole at the time, Moore hid the body and returned a while later to mutilate it so it could not be identified. He was arrested for the crime a month later and told the police his side of the story. He said that he had shot Brueck by accident and that he had died immediately, that he, Moore, knew just having the gun would land him back in jail and that he mutilated the body to stay out of the penitentiary.

The Shelby County prosecutor's office reconstructed the crime differently. They said that Moore had kidnapped Brueck and had premeditated the murder. A year after the crime Mike Moore was tried for first-degree murder plus kidnapping, was convicted and sentenced to die. In June 1979 he was given a stay of execution only a week before his scheduled electrocution. His appeal of his conviction is at present before the Tennessee Supreme Court.

Mike Moore describes himself as the black sheep of a solidly middle-class family. His parents moved often while he grew up but he spent most of his high school years in Memphis. He says that his gullibility and weakness for peer pressure led him to trouble in high school and beyond. He went directly from high school to the Army and Vietnam.

His record in Vietnam was good and his survival there noteworthy. A large percentage of the people he went to Vietnam with never made it back. He speaks of his experience there as a frenzied stay, a "weird" time of aimless action and senseless death. He returned, got out of the Army and went to college.

In college he was no model of diligence, but he made it through two years of a sociology course at Memphis State. He started spending more time playing cards than going to class and in a short while was in trouble. He was arrested for and convicted of second-degree burglary and arson. He says that he drove a friend to the friend's girlfriend's house but was not aware the friend was going to burglarize and set fire to it. Moore spent three years in the state prison on that conviction.

Released from prison, he quickly married and worked as a truck driver. His life, however, was far from settled. He says his house was the local gathering point for impromptu parties and drinking sprees. His motorcycles became an obsession and that obsession plus his many days away from Memphis ruined his marriage. In the summer of 1977 his wife moved back to her parents and he moved into a house with a friend. The parties continued until Chuck Brueck's death.

Mike Moore is a tall man who was probably once lean and muscular. Two years behind bars have given him a bit too much weight and a sag that he himself laments. His spirit, though, has not followed his body's lead. He seems jaunty and whimsical at times with a locker-room sort of banter. Keeping his sense of humor, he explained, is necessary for his survival.

It is easy for us to misconstrue a sense of humor on death row as callousness. From the outside we expect the condemned to be in a constant state of serious remorse. That, of course, is impossible. My visit to Tennessee's death row lasted over several days and included one whole day on the row itself. Those days were most instructive as to how someone survives a sentence of death.

Newly painted a chocolate brown with yellow walls and ceiling and red floors, the ten cells that make up Tennessee's death row are one door away from the electric chair. That door dominates the row and effectively mutes the new paint job. The door does not silence conversation, however. While guards took inmates one at a time to shower and while deliverers from the mess hall shoved plastic trays of food under the cell doors, the ten men shouted shorthand bits of talk to each other. The joking that went on in that talk was the good-natured kidding of young men, the kind you might find at five o'clock in a working-class bar, mixed with some gallows humor that I suspected might have been for my benefit. Given the surroundings the normalcy of the give and take was noticeable. The joking, I came to see, was not that of people laughing at their captors or sloughing off the seriousness of their crimes, but was one way those ten men assured themselves they were still alive.

Mike Moore says that he has told the truth, that he has done so, with a few exceptions, from the beginning and that others have lied to make the death seem purposeful and more brutal than it was. He says that his reward for telling the truth has been the most severe sentence possible, death. He expresses sorrow for the killing and the pain it brought Brueck's family but his remorse is qualified. He feels violated by a system of justice that asked him to tell the truth and sentenced him to death for doing so. The cynicism engendered by this felt injustice seems to be winning Moore's attention more often than remorse for the death as days and months on death row stretch into years.

Moore says that the electric chair does not yet bother him and won't until his time comes. What bothers him now is that his story has not been believed and, to his way of thinking, simply because he chose to cooperate, the tragedy of Chuck Brueck's death may be compounded by his own.

I WAS BORN in Mobile in '49. My daddy was in the Border Patrol at the time. I have a brother and a sister. We moved a lot, San Antonio, St. Louis until '64 and then my father retired from the border patrol and we moved back to Memphis. I enjoyed the moving and traveling. My Mom and Dad used to travel all over the United States showing dogs. I just loved it.

*You were a close family?*
Always been. I was always the black sheep of the family but they stuck by me all the way.

*How were you the black sheep of the family?*
Well, my sister, she got her college degree and she's working for the Governor's office in the state of Washington. My brother is the vice president of the international division of a bank. Here I am sort of the dummy of the group. But they've been good to me, even though I got in trouble a few years ago. They stuck by me all the way to the end. There wasn't any time in my life that my family and I had any type of problems.

*Yours was a typical middle-class family? You never lacked for money or anything you wanted?*
I always wanted a pony but I never got it! Seriously, I didn't know whether things were tight when I was growing up or not. But I'd say Mom and Dad were pretty well off. I mean, I never had to worry about anything. They're not destitute or anything. They're not filthy rich either.

*Did you have a rough time in high school?*
That's a yes and no. I was doing pretty good in high school and I was playing sports all through, football, baseball, basketball. It was in '66; I didn't make the football team that year, the varsity team, but I made varsity basketball. When I didn't make the football team it gave me more time to myself, I guess. That's when I started noticing girls and I started wanting to please them and impress them. I started partying a lot, getting drunk. I didn't care. Everybody's getting drunk, so I got drunk.

I guess that's where my problems started. I just followed the group to be accepted. Back then I was real naive. Somebody could tell me something and I'd say, "Oh, wow." I'd believe it. I know I was real naive about a lot of things that were going on. I don't think drugs were that big back then, 'cause if they were, they weren't on my level. I got suspended a couple of times in high school, a couple of fights and stuff like this. My biggie in high school was this one: (this is how naive I was) somebody told me that if you take a cherry bomb and you drop it down the commode and flush it, it'll explode and smoke will come out. I thought that would be pretty neat so I went to the gym with the silly thing, hit the plunger, threw it and it didn't go down. It just went bing, bing, bing and bounced around that bowl. I saw the fuse getting shorter and shorter and I said, "It's time for me to get out of here." I just turned and started going out the stall door when the thing blew up, showered me with water and porcelain. I came staggering out of there and I couldn't hear a thing. I snuck out but the next day they expelled me. Mom and Dad were mad and upset but they were still with me.

I got transferred to a different high school. I cleaned up my act a little bit there. I was ineligible for sports because of the transfer so I went out for the ROTC drill team. I finally made it out of high school and went into the service, the Army.

Through basic and advanced infantry training I was a squad leader. Then in Vietnam, Bien Ho Province, again I was a squad leader. It was a long range patrol group, search and destroy. We were more like the advanced scouting platoon for the 82nd airborne armored group. We'd stay one to two weeks in the field and we'd see where the forces were and then we'd figure out how we were gonna maneuver from there.

*Did you ever get into heavy combat?*
You can't stay over there and not get into some kind of heavy combat if you're on the front line group. It gets heavy from time to time on night patrols. You run into booby traps and before you know it you hear fire fighting. All you see is fire flashing and bullets zinging. You hear people scream and you don't know what's going on. Most of the guys stayed bombed out of their heads so a fire bomb like that happens and you go, "Wow, man, look at the colors."

*Did you get into that yourself, were you into drugs over there?*
Well it beat the whiskey over there. They did weird things with that whiskey. Drugs were about the safest thing to do.

*Did you see many of your friends die?*

Yes, I did. In one platoon I was in we had about 50 men in that platoon and during the entire time over there eight of us made it back. Some were wounded, some weren't. But, of course, much of it was carelessness. You get too smashed and you go out there and stumble into a pit or some of the booby traps they got. It was weird. We would have to call all our artillery in on our position, almost on top of us, so we could haul our butts out of there a little bit and get back to a landing site where a chopper could come and pick us up.

*How long were you in the Army?*

Close to three years. I was in Vietnam one year, a little over one year.

*And when you got out?*

When I got out I went to school, Memphis State University. I completed two years in sociology and got a certificate. Then I started hanging out in the student center and playing cards all day long. That started getting me in trouble with my teachers because I wasn't going to class. Peer pressure is probably one of the worst things in the world. Nobody wants to be an outcast. But it's kind of crazy, things people do to be accepted.

*What happened?*

I got charged on second-degree burglary and arson in '72, was convicted and got three years.

*What was that all about?*

A friend of mine was dating this girl out in Germantown and her parents found out he wasn't the good guy he was telling everybody he was supposed to have been. They just said he couldn't see their daughter. So he asked me to take him out to her house cause he wanted to talk to her, he wanted to get his ring back and all. I took him out there and he went in through the garage. He was gone five or six minutes and when he got back he said, "That's it." The next day the Germantown police department called and said they wanted to see me. Sure enough the place had been burglarized and set on fire. I just told them what happened. My friend said I did this and this and I kept trying to state what had happened. But the jury went ahead and found me guilty. We both went to the penal farm but, strange thing, I got transferred to the penitentiary here.

I was granted parole once and I had a sixty day wait before my papers came back. I was seeing this girl and we went ahead and got married without permission. I figured sixty days, big deal. The State of Tennessee didn't look at it that way. They declined me my parole. I had to do the whole three years. August 21, 1975 Mom came up and picked me up. It felt good to be back.

My counselor and my parole officer did me a favor. They told this employer in Memphis I was doing all over-the-road-driving for the State of Tennessee and got me a job. So I started driving. I never drove a tractor trailer before in my life. I had gotten a cheap divorce while I was still in the penitentiary. And then in 1976 I married a different lady.

The first day I was out of prison they gave me something like $30 and a bus ticket. So I took the $30 and bought two lids of grass and I went straight out to this lake that I go fishing at a lot. I figured I'd do some fishing and got high. I got my line tangled up and everything. The work, the driving, was easy. I got free vacations just about. I could drive wherever I wanted to go and get paid for it. The money was good and the working conditions were good. All I did was drive a truck and so I had my fun.

I thought marriage was going to settle me down a bit. It didn't. I partied more when I was married than when I was single. There were people in that house almost twenty-four hours a day. If it wasn't our friends it was our neighbors and if it wasn't our neighbors it was my mother-in-law. We'd have a bunch of people over there and they'd all be stoned and then all of a sudden you hear a car door and I look out, "It's your mother!" and everything gets shoved underneath couches and deodorant sprayed all through the house.

No, I sure didn't settle down. I started pouring all my money into this motorcycle I had. Oh, my wife hated that. I'd get out there with a cooler, buy a case of beer and just sit down on the cooler, work on the bike, get drunk. If I finished working on the bike I'd go ride it. If I didn't I'd just drink until I'd fall on the ground.

My wife liked to party. I couldn't keep up with her. And with my driving on the road and all like this I guess she felt neglected. I know she felt neglected. She was going to school. We just kept having problems. She went home to mama and I got stuck with the apartment to take care of. That's when I started with this certain crowd. That's when I met Chuck, the boy that got killed. He stayed at my apartment for a while. When the landlord complained about the rent I just up and left. Left them holding the bag on that. So Vince, the guy who was charged in this case with me as an accessory, and I moved into a house. That was back in the last part of July, '77. We didn't stay there too long.

*And what happened?*

In October of '77 I was arrested.

*And you admitted that you killed Chuck?*

I shot the boy, yes but I didn't murder the boy. We were out near the railroad tracks and we had a pistol. During one of the times I was handing the pistol back, I wasn't paying attention and I'm sure he wasn't either. The pistol went off and the bullet went through the left side of his arm and into his chest. When he fell he grabbed his left arm with his right hand and I thought he got shot in the arm. It still scared the hell out of me 'cause I couldn't believe what was going on. He just fell down and I went over. I saw a lot of blood between his chest and his arm so I moved his right arm away and lifted his left arm up. When I did I saw all this blood coming out of his chest. He just looked up at me and said, "Fudley, get me a doctor." And right after he said that, he died. I tried to get a pulse and there was no pulse. There was no breathing, or at least no breathing that I could tell, so I got up and I started heading down the railroad tracks.

I got about fifty feet away from the body and I looked back and saw this body lying there. I knew if I saw it somebody else would. It was freaking me out. So, dumb me, not knowing what was going on too well, I had two shots left and all I wanted to do was get rid of the gun. So I may have emptied those two shells into the body. I went back and dumped the body off the bridge, drug him into the woods and then I went back and told my roommate what happened. I'm not used to shooting friends.

*Why would you put those other two bullets into the body?*

I hate to say it but right now I don't know. I had so many things running through my mind at the time. Everybody asks me, "Why didn't you call the police right then?" I was a convicted ex-felon. I had a pistol in my possession. I think it's an automatic five-year sentence if an ex-felon is found with a pistol in his possession. I wasn't ready to go back to prison for another five years. I don't think anybody is.

So I went home and told my roommate. That didn't help him any. He sort of went to pieces. He was going out with his girlfriend and he said, "I'm gonna be back at 11:00. When I come back, take my car, go down there at midnight and cut the boy's head off," cause he knew that he could be identified by his teeth. I didn't know what to do. We just talked about it and talked about it and a couple of days went by. He just decided that the teeth had to go. So he got his shotgun and he told me to get a shovel. We got in his car and went out there and shot his teeth out and covered him up, cause I told him I didn't want him to be hidden or anything like this. I said, "I'd like him to be found." I wanted the boy to get a funeral or at least be found, be taken care of, the body taken care of.

So we just covered him up. Of course animals had already eaten on him and there was bugs all over him. We left. I got a phone call at 10:00 on October 7th in the morning saying that Homicide was coming out that night and arresting me for the murder of Chuck Brueck. I knew well in advance that the police were coming. If I was guilty of murder or worried about getting convicted of murder, I would have gone a long time before that, or when I heard that. But I figured if they came in I was gonna tell them what happened and just get it off my chest. I got rid of the pistol. I gave it to this guy. He took care of it for me and Homicide came out and arrested me under investigation of homicide. They questioned me and questioned me that night and I didn't answer any of the questions. A friend of mine who was a civil suit lawyer at the time was just there on the spur of the moment just to act as legal counsel until he could get somebody from his firm in criminal law to come in and take over. The next morning they brought me in and they wouldn't let me see my attorney. They kept telling me that my attorneys weren't gonna be there, that they didn't want to get involved in this type of thing and so on and so on. So I just went ahead and told them what had happened, at least what I could remember. Right after we got past the incriminating part they stopped the investigation. A few minutes later my friend the attorney came in with one of his associates and they said they had been waiting out there all the time, waiting for me to get brought up. They didn't even know I was in the interrogation room. After the lawyer read what was already said, he said there was nothing they could do to actually help me. They said maybe they could see what they could do on a plea bargain. But I told them, "Well, thank you," and all this and I just went on back down and I've been locked up here since.

*You expected a death penalty conviction?*

No. Not really. Under the evidence that they had I wasn't expecting a guilty verdict on first degree murder at all. I was pretty sure that with the evidence that I knew they had before the trial that even a guilty verdict on second-degree murder wouldn't happen either. But when court time came, things changed. They had about five or six witnesses who lied their little butts off on the stand. They had these two boys who swore up and down that I pulled a gun on the boy, kidnapped him from his house and drove off. But yet those two boys, when they said they saw me kidnap him, they didn't call the police. They didn't even call the boy's mother till after the body was found and that was a good month later.

*That was the aggravating circumstance then, kidnapping?*

They had to prove kidnapping in order to show premeditation. They said I killed him because I was supposed to be the biggest marijuana dealer in Memphis. If I was the biggest marijuana dealer in Memphis I sure wouldn't have had the lawyer I had. I would have had a better attorney than him.

*How do you feel about the crime now?*

My roommate will tell you and the people who were close to me at the time will tell you I was really shook up. I mean the boy was a friend. It wasn't a stranger or somebody I hated. That might have been a different story. But it was somebody that I knew intimately. We shared an apartment. We partied together. His girlfriend would come over, my girlfriend would come over, things like that. So we got to know each other on a one-to-one basis. I liked Chuck. He was a good friend. And I guess the way that I knew him and to know that he died because of me, it's a thing that shook me up more than, say, the legal aspect of it. I felt sick and sorry. I felt remorse for what happened. But after what I've gone through, right now I could care less.

*What do you mean?*

I didn't murder the boy and I'm on death row. I got convicted for something I did not do. So, I mean, what am I gonna do say, "Oh, wow, I forgive you all and I love you all?" It's hard for me to say that. I know it put the Brueck's through a lot of hell and pain because Chuck died. I'm not dismissing that. But in the same light also, it didn't do my family any good either for the first-degree murder conviction plus the death penalty sentence. I'm not saying one outweighs the other. I'm not saying that everybody is using or exploiting the death of Chuck Brueck for their own reasons. But there are a few who are and that is the thing that's changing my entire thinking about the case, or at least about the death.

*What was it like, then, once you got the death penalty?*

I was prepared for the worst so when they came back and gave me death I could handle it. And then after everything was said and done the jury went out, the case was closed and I looked over to my mama. She didn't come for the whole trial except for that damn sentencing. When they came back with death it tore her up. It tore my father and brother up. For my own sanity I wanted to get my brother, father and mother out of there. One of the bailiffs who was real good to me all through the trial said it'd probably be better if I went ahead and left. So I went on back down. It took me a few minutes to sort of pull myself back together and get myself mentally psyched up. I got back upstairs and everybody wanted to know what happened. I told them. They were freaking out and I was able to handle it. I'm still able to handle it. I had a lot of friends like that old counselor I had when I was in prison before. He came to see me. He couldn't understand why I wasn't crying or had gray hair or was not coming out in a straightjacket or something like this. I was joking around and laughing. He kept saying, "You got the death penalty, you ought to be worried." And I said, "It's not gonna do me any good to worry."

*Say a little more about that. I think most people feel like your counselor does.*

Well is it gonna do me any good if I let it worry me and destroy me mentally, emotionally, spiritually? No. I'm not gonna just let it dominate my entire behavioral process. We make jokes. We kid about it. After John Spenkelink's execution in Florida it had us concerned but it does not have us worried or scared or anything like that. It just brings out some concern that, OK, it happened in Florida, we know it can also happen here, but we feel pretty sure that it won't.

*You must have some times when it's not that certain in your mind.*

I had a June 29, 1979 date set and did not get a stay of execution until a week before that. I had been on death row here since January trying to get something done on my case so I could go ahead and get the stay. All these fools were waiting to the last minute to get something done. I've got a bad stomach now and a few more gray hairs.

Actually it wasn't dominating my whole thought process. I knew it was there but I didn't let it bother me that much. Of course the guys on the walk joked around and stuff like this. "Hey I hear they're working back there on your chair, boy." We kid about the chair and stuff like this. They bring tours back there and we yell, "Hey Richard, you'd better tell them to stay away from your chair." Of course to us it's funny. People on the street—it's probably not that funny to them.

*What's the reason for the jokes?*

Well the humor picks up your spirits and your emotions. If you can laugh about it, it helps alleviate any fear or uncertainty or any type of concern. It just helps to kick it off in a corner for a while and you sort of go back and you feel a little lighter.

*What about those times when you can't kick it back in the corner?*

I don't have that problem.

*But it hasn't become real for you, has it?*

The day they take me out of cell six and take me back to cell ten and shave my head and my legs, I think it's gonna become a problem then. I think at that time I'm gonna start worrying. Really worrying. But until then it's not gonna do me any good, it's not gonna do nobody any good just to sit back and worry about it cause the problem's not that imminent yet.

*I imagine that a majority of people who heard about your case agreed with the jury that you should be executed. Why do you think that might be?*

The only thing that society, John Q. Public, knows about what has happened is what the prosecution has said and what the papers have said. Of course the business of the papers is selling papers. If they bring out the gory side of it and not bring out, say, the other half of it, they're gonna sell more papers with the gory side than they are with, say, the real side, the full account of what happened. So John Q. Public, he sees only one aspect of it and that is the grotesque part, the cruel, the cold part of it. And sure John Q. Public is gonna say, "That boy deserves the chair." But if they were to see the entire scope of what has transpired, I don't think the public or society or anybody would be ready to jump off and say, "Give him the chair."

My Dad's told me to tell the truth. Only good can come out of it. And I did basically, except in areas like drinking and smoking reefer that my attorney warned me not to say anything about. My attorney wanted me to say that I shot the boy once, that how the other slugs got there I didn't know and all this. But on the stand when it got to that point I went ahead and told him about it. I had it on my chest for the longest time and I wanted to get it off. It was just something I had to do.

I could have kept quiet and shut up all through the investigation, not told them where the pistol was or anything like this. There would be no way in the world they could prove anything with no pistol, no collaborating statements. I could have played games with the police and tried to walk away from the whole thing. But it was just something that I felt needed to be done, telling the truth. I don't know how to explain this. There was a conflict inside of me. I did something wrong and I admit it. The boy was a friend of mine, a close friend. I didn't mean that he would die and that happened out of ignorance and stupidity. So in telling the truth I thought I was doing right, I thought it was the right thing to do.

# Charles Young Jr.

Charles Young Jr.'s life is pinned to December 15, 1975. Every thought he has these days, every move he makes, every letter he writes is in some way connected to that date. He does not allow himself to forget it for a moment. It was, he says, the date he first fired a handgun. It was the date of his first arrest and the start of his first experience with courts and the legal system. And, he says over and over again, it was the date that he became responsible for the death of another man.

On December 15, 1975 Charles Young Jr., twenty eight years old at the time and unemployed, killed Ruben Flynt at his home in Union Point, Georgia. Ruben Flynt, a white man, was the vice-president of a local bank that Charles Young and his family used often. Charles was arrested the day of the murder, confessed to the crime saying that it occurred during an argument, and, three months later, was convicted of first-degree murder and sentenced to die in Georgia's electric chair at the state prison in Reidsville. His appeal of that sentence has gone all the way to the U.S. Supreme Court and has been denied throughout.

Union Point, Georgia, is a crossroads in Greene County, a sparsely populated county that encompasses the Oconee National Forest in north central Georgia. A capital offense in Union Point is a rare occurrence. Ruben Flynt's murder received much local press coverage. His position in the bank and the fact that he was killed in his home by a black man made the crime a very frightening one to the people of the county. The jury in the case, presented with little evidence to the contrary, believed the prosecutor's reconstruction of the murder that Charles Young Jr. plotted Ruben Flynt's death and did not kill him in an argument, as Young claims.

Sentencing in first-degree murder cases is variable. A crime that receives the death penalty in one part of the state may very well receive a life sentence in another part of the state. Specifically, rural counties are much more likely to sentence people to death than are urban centers. In Charles Young Jr.'s case it could be argued that had he committed the crime for which he now sits on death row in Atlanta instead of Union Point, he might not now be facing the electric chair.

But that variable does not seem to bother Young. At one point in our talk he said that he and he alone was to blame for being in the position he is in and that he could not fault errors in the judgment against him when he was the reason for the judgment being made in the first place. He does not feel he should die. He does not believe in capital punishment. He hopes only that his side of the story will be heard.

Young applies that sort of even-handed approach to his original lawyer, who, it is alleged in his present appeals, did much less than he should have to represent his client. Though Young's family hired him thinking he was a good criminal lawyer it appears that his experience with the new death penalty laws was limited. Though Young was a family man with a wife and two children, had attended college, and had never before been arrested for anything, his lawyer presented none of that evidence as mitigating factors in the sentencing phase of the trial. In fact at one point in the guilt-innocence phase of the trial it became obvious to the judge and the prosecutor that he didn't know there was to be a separate sentencing phase of the trial.

Though Young is understandably critical of his original lawyer and the errors he made, he is not bitter about it. He feels that the best he can do now is to be as aware of his legal situation as is possible from his death row cell.

Young is kept at the Georgia Diagnostic and Classification Center in Jackson, Georgia, halfway between Atlanta and Macon. A modern prison completed in 1969, it looks to be at least fifty percent underground. The majority of death row prisoners in Georgia are at Reidsville. The prison in Jackson holds the overflow.

Inmates at Jackson wear crisp white uniforms with navy blue collars on the shirts and a white navy blue stripe down the pant leg. Charles Young Jr. is a thin man of medium height who wears this uniform with style. We talked in a small maximum security visiting room. An assistant superintendant of the prison stayed in the room with us the whole time. His presence did not seem to bother Young.

He talks slowly and deliberately with a deep resonant voice that rolled around the concrete blocks of the visiting room and at times, during the difficult parts of our conversation, dropped to a bass whisper. Our interview was long but he never lost his concentration. It was clear that much of the time in his cell is spent going over the things we talked about.

Because of an agreement with Young's lawyer we did not discuss the specifics of the crime though he made it clear that his reconstruction of the killing differed completely from that of the prosecution. Young did not, however, sidestep his responsibility for Ruben Flynt's death. In fact he seemed nearly consumed by it. I asked few questions as we talked. Young delivered a monologue. When the assistant superintendant told us our time was up Young got up from the table and, shaking my hand, told me just how weary he was and what a toll on him his time in prison has been. I imagined that he would return to his cell and continue his monologue to himself long after my tape recorder clicked off.

I HAD NEVER been in a situation like this before. I was just kind of in another world after what happened. I was really shocked by what transpired that day. How could a day that started out so beautifully. . . . it looked like it was the most beautiful day of my life . . . I'll never forget it. The sun was out, the temperature was in the seventies on December 15, 1975.

The more I look at it it seems the biggest mistake that I made was trying to tell the truth on the day that this crime occurred. They asked me did I want an attorney. So I said, "Yeah." They said well it would be the next day before they could get an attorney for me but you can talk to us and anything that you say is confidential. So they explained this and so basically I was truthful with them about the things they were asking. But once we finished they asked me to sign the statement. I didn't sign the statement. I felt that the lawyer should have a chance to look at it. But anyway I did basically try to tell the truth about the thing. I find now that if I had not made a statement, if I had not talked with those people, they would never have misconstrued the things I was trying to be honest with them about.

*Tell me what did happen on December 15, 1975?*

I was charged with murder, armed robbery and robbery by intimidation on December 15, 1975. On February 19, 1976 I was sentenced to death for the murder, life for robbery and twenty years for the robbery by intimidation.

But it really goes back a year or so before that. I went down to Union Point and I got one loan for $3500 dollars. My wife's grandparents had given us a house in Greene County and we were going to sell the house and pay off the loan that way. When we weren't able to sell the house I went back and had it refinanced. This man at the bank that redid the loan, named Conger or Cogginger, we had him do it because the man we usually see, Mr. Flynt, was out of the bank that day.

It was about a year after that that Mr. Flynt was in the bank one day and my grandmother and I went down to see him. I borrowed two thousand dollars that day and he was telling us that the insurance on the first loan was not properly done. So I told him that day at the bank that I would never deal with any other person in that bank. Every time we went to the bank it was to see Mr. Flynt.

So on December 15, I went down, I drove by the bank and I didn't see Mr. Flynt's car. I was thinking I was behind in the loan but, without me knowing it, the loan had been transferred to my grandmother. She was the co-signer on the loan.

I drove over to Mr. Flynt's house, parked, went there to his door. He came to the door and said, "Well just go on back down to the bank. I'll be back down there in a minute." And I told him I was in a rush because my cousin, I had his car and he was looking for me back when he got off from work. I was really running late.

So I told him I'd like to call my grandmother. I went in and tried but the line was busy. So we continued to talk there and he was cooking. I never will forget, he was cooking. Cooking a hamburger or something. I don't know exactly what it was. So he was telling me that I didn't have the loans, that the loans had been transferred to my grandmother and that's when things got out of hand. My grandmother does not work, she's worked in her life but she has no way to be paying my bills and supporting me.

*What was the state's theory about the crime?*

The theory the state used against me was that I had conspired to go down and kill this man. Anybody that knows me or knows my family knew that I had no reason, no earthly reason whatsoever to go and rob nobody. My grandmother has always, if I had needed the money, wanted the money, I could have gotten it. As far as my going out having to rob, kill, steal. I had no reason whatsoever to do that.

I'm not so cold-hearted or so bloodthirsty or money-thirsty that I would want something like that to happen. And even right now, at this point in time, if I have to go to the chair, I just have to go to the chair. I believe that will be God's will, you know. If I go I go. But I don't want to go and I surely didn't want to mess my life up like this. And I didn't want to cause his family the grief that they've had to go through.

*Your appeal has gone all the way to the Supreme Court. What is your appeal based on?*

At this time I think my appeals are being based on my counsel. There were a lot of errors and things that happened in the trial. I had no idea of the type of representation I was getting. I've had to ask and I've read in briefs where the court has upheld my sentence. They state flatly why didn't I file here and why didn't I do this. I had no idea what he was going to do or what his trial strategy was. My people paid him quite a bit of money to represent me there in Greene County.

I never was just able to sit down and tell him what happened, try to explain to him what happened. I never got that chance with him. He came over and stayed about ten or fifteen minutes. He was so hyped up over these news articles and everything. He's saying it's looking bad. And he never sat down and I never got a chance to really basically explain to him what happened on December 15, 1975.

And him being, I guess, from the old school, he was dead set on believing that if a black guy killed a man down here in a county like this he had to be crazy. And so we filed a special plea of insanity. He waived it the morning they're going to hear it.

We presented no evidence at all in the sentencing phase of the trial. They were going out to bring back sho' enough life or death, you know, and he presented nothing! The records show that he presented nothing at all in the sentencing phase of the trial. When it came to mitigating and aggravating circumstances there should have been some emphasis placed on the fact that I had never been arrested, had never had a criminal record, nothing but a minor traffic violation.

I don't want nobody to think that I'm going to walk out of prison. I feel that I should pay a price for what transpired. The point about being guilty or innocent is just a concrete fact. But I did not conspire. I hadn't plotted this man's death. And the records show that my lawyer presented nothing at all in the sentencing phase of the trial.

I didn't know that I could get up and fire him if I wanted. All I knew was that I went in the courtroom, that my family's gone and done got what I thought was a good lawyer. But after I read the transcript of the trial and I'm made aware of errors by briefs and things that have been filed, I find out that maybe he wasn't as good as my people thought. To this day he doesn't have in his file, in any files, a complete statement from me about what actually happened that day.

*Tell me something about your people, where you grew up.*

I was born in Fulton County and lived in Fulton County for about ninety days. My parents, you know, they busted up, or what have you, and my mother carried me to my grandmother there in Greene County. I lived with her and my grandfather there. My grandfather passed, I believe it was '56 when he died. My grandmother continued to bring me up. I went to high school there.

*Did you keep in touch with your mother and father during that time?*

My Mom, she'd come down some. My Dad came sometimes. Not nothing on a regular basis. I saw him I guess four times before I got 18 years old.

I had uncles and aunts. They're just like my mother and dad. I grew up at my grandmother's place and my uncle lived there and his sons and aunt and all. We all lived together, one big family and everything. The two sons and I went to high school together and like if their mom and pop bought them a pair of sneakers, for Joe Jr. and Willy Daniel, they bought a pair of sneakers for me.

It just seemed as if, you know, there was something kind of missing growing up. You see these guys at basketball games, football games, track meets or baseball games and your father's not there. It's kind of like a missing element, missing part of your life. Even though I understand it. It might have been circumstances and things at the time. I don't know what the relationship between them was. I really don't know what brought about the change and why they separated and stuff like that. Really never wanted to know. I never blamed them. I don't blame them for my being here. I can't blame. I can't point my finger at them. I can't blame nobody for being here. I blame me.

As far as my background and my bringing up I think that I was disciplined, well disciplined. I think that I was taught respect. You respect yourself and you respect others. You just don't go around pointing a finger at other people. You just don't blame other people for your downfalls. You got to face the music. If you made it hard you lay in it. That's what they told me. As bad as I would hate to go to Reidsville to be executed I would go down there if it came to that. I'd go.

I did pretty good in high school. I was a pretty active youth and stuff, participated in sports. Most of the people in the black community that was about anything knew me. They had known me for quite a while. They knew that I never did nothing. I wasn't allowed to go out and stay all night when I was eighteen years old.

I graduated from high school and went to Clarke Community College. I didn't do anything at Clarke. I was just throwing away my grandmother's money. I told her I didn't want to go to school right then but she insisted. I felt like, you know, after having gone through high school and everything I just wanted a break. I begged her. And my grandmother, she didn't let me. Her and my mama all crying and all wanting me to go to school. So I went on. But as far as giving my best, I didn't. And the record will show that I didn't.

And I always felt guilty about it. Especially now I feel guilty, even more guilty about that because I look at it for what it was. Out of all the people in my life I would have to say that my grandmother was the strongest force in my life. She wanted me to do well. She gave everything for me.

I met my wife in high school. I was a junior in high school

when I met her. That was 1964. We were married in '66. I went off from high school and I hadn't been used to fooling around with a lot of girls and things. I guess I kind of went through a change in my life. It wasn't that I lost my sense of value or my sense of where I wanted to go in life. It was just that all through high school I come home, I make an A, and anything less than that is not going to be good enough. Joe Jr. and Willie Daniel didn't make the grades that I made. Well, after so many years of being the pacesetter I was really ready to unwind, at least for a year after I finished high school.

*Do you have children?*

I have two kids. Charles, he'll be thirteen the 28th of November. My daughter Katrice she was eleven this past March 15th. I think about my family as well as the Flynt family. And when I pray, I pray for my family as well as the victim's family. I haven't just destroyed my future or my life, I've destroyed my family to a certain extent. Each day that I sit here on death row, each day that I've been locked up, I've caused them pain. They still care about me and it just continues to eat away.

Just the first of this year I went through one of the roughest periods of time in my life. I still haven't healed from it yet. My wife chose to divorce me. It was kinda like being executed when I found out she wanted a divorce. I could have said, "Hey don't do this to me now. I'm down. My back is against the wall. Here I am facing death. God, no, don't you pull out too. Hey, don't leave now. If you leave me now like my whole world and everything is just going to crash. This is it right here, you know. Don't, don't please." But I chose not to contest this, not even to sit her down and try to convince her. I sit here in a situation where I don't have a secure future to offer her or my children. And my children are at an age where they need their father to be with them. They need guidance. They're coming into the stage where they really need somebody to be with 'em. And I thought in my own way that the divorce was my way of telling my wife that I wanted her to be happy no matter what, even though I wasn't able to do it for her or give 'em this life or my kids a secure future.

I still have her on the visiting list here and everything because if she wants to come and bring the children I want her always to be able to come. After I had come up here she really hadn't come often here because each time she came and left it was too painful. The last time she came here, in December of '77, and brought the children and she was leaving it was just something like hey, good God, I couldn't help but cry. I cried before she left, I cried on the way back to the cell, I cried after I got in the cell because I looked at them, you know, they having to go one way and my having to go back another, knowing I was the cause of it all.

*What about Mr. Flynt's family? Did you ever have any dealings with them after the trial?*

I pray for them. I've been sitting here thinking how I would approach them if I could approach them. I want to approach them. Then again I don't know how to approach them. Here in a situation like this if you approach them people will say well you're trying to save your neck. In the courtroom that night I told them I didn't want to bring no harm to any family. I didn't want to bring no bad times, no hurt. I wouldn't want to go to them now or write 'em or what have you. I wouldn't want them thinking, "He's just trying to save his neck."

I'm not so cold-hearted, so vicious, so bloodthirsty, such a robber and killer and stuff. I'm no Jesse James. I know I'm not like that. And I never will be no matter what. But in this situation I know that they have a right to have hard feelings toward me. I know. I expect that. If I don't get any relief one of the last things I would want to say would be to state to them how sorry I am about what happened. I'd want them to know it.

*How has this been for your grandmother?*

My grandmother's got in bad health and I worry about her a lot. She was by to see me maybe a month or so ago. I believe it was the Saturday before or something like that. I was glad to be able to see her. She's seventy-eight years old now. She's gone through a lot. Even though she comes in and tries to make me happy and everything I know this right here has been a great, great, great burden on her.

*What do you do here in prison?*

I had an extension course I was taking from a seminary. I write people all over the state. I write maybe sixty, seventy people, something like that, plus my family. I found a lot of love, a lot of prayers, a lot of hope by writing and communicating with these people. And it's given me a lot of strength, like back in June when they denied me certiorari in the U.S. Supreme Court.

*What's it been like going through the appeals procedure?*

I've had so many setbacks. The lawyer is telling you you got a chance, you got it down on paper. But it just doesn't seem to pan out when the ruling comes down.

I guess when this first started and I started receiving the

rejection I had really a lot of hope, hoping that things might turn, not necessarily peaches and ice cream, but I was hoping that things might turn a little bit and I'd get some kind of relief.

You're tried and you come out of the county and you go in the Georgia Supreme Court on automatic appeal. Alright that appeal is denied. O.K., well, you say you won't give up hope. This is the first step right here. I don't give up hope. All right you go into habeus corpus or whatever and you're denied, you go into U.S. Supreme Court and you're denied and all this is piling up and in the meantime you're losing your wife, your family and everything is just going haywire.

After so many rejections each time it takes a little bit more and a little bit more. You have to reach really down inside to come up with the strength to continue. You look around you at cases. You know the swiftness that they are being upheld and the manner in which they are being handled and it kind of takes away from what little hope that you have. I find each day is getting a little bit tougher. A little bit tougher to get up and get ready to try to do it. Like I say I write letters and I share with people. I feel like I gain a lot from writing people. It's kind of like travel. It's good therapy because I wouldn't go up there and tell the guard, "Hey I got a headache. I want to sit down and talk with you."

*In June of '77 you had a date set. How close did you come to being executed?*

Too close. It was my understanding it was a matter of hours when I got this stay of execution, before I was to be executed. Now at this time my life is in other people's hands, the lawyer, my family and what have you. My life depends on what other people can do for me. It's very important my being able to communicate with these people and kind of keep up with what's happening and what's going on in my case. Back in 1976 I went in the courtroom just sitting there, not really knowing what's what. But now I have to know about what's going to be done next. When the date was set in '77 I had my original lawyer and I found out about the date over the radio, over the news. And that's why I'm very, very timid and very self-conscious about a date being set on me because I want to know what's going to be done to try to keep this from happening.

*Do you think executing you would be unjust?*

Well this is the way I feel about it. Quite naturally I don't support capital punishment. And I guess most people, if they would read up in a paper or see a comment by me or anybody else in this position that said they didn't believe in capital punishment, would say, "Well he's got a pretty darn good reason for not believing in capital punishment!" But I think that society is more advanced than capital punishment. Even if you had people that you feel you couldn't control there are different ways and different things that could be done. There are many things that could be done that could help people in deterring them other than saying that capital punishment is a deterrent. Capital punishment is really not a deterrent. I think it can only serve as a hindrance to society because society is greater than capital punishment.

*You've spoken of God and prayer some. Could you say something about your beliefs?*

I do believe in God. I believed in God when I went to church before I came to prison. I didn't just start to believe when I got here. I had strayed away some before coming. I guess now after being here and going through this experience and continuing to be here under this type sentence my belief has been strengthened. I do believe it takes more than human love to sustain me during times like these. And deep down inside I know it's been the strength and the love and the help of God that's carried me this far. I believe he'll continue to carry me and sustain me although I don't know what he might do with me.

It's just gotten to the point now I'm physically tired. And I'm mentally tired. It takes so much to try to continue on under these conditions. I feel tired, very tired. I really don't know where it will all end. I'm just trying to prepare myself for whatever comes.

# Johnny "Imani" Harris

We spoke in the starkest of surroundings: a room at the end of the segregation wing of Holman Prison, one of two prisons near Atmore, Alabama. A table and two chairs had been set out for the interview. The room had no electrical outlets, no wastebasket. One half of one wall of the room was glass, mesh-reinforced glass, a prison staple. Beyond the glass we could see another room, a door to the left, a small platform in the middle of the room and a bright yellow, heavy, square, wooden object on the platform. We were in the witness room; the yellow object was Alabama's electric chair.

It was brought over from the old Kilby prison and given a new coat of paint about four years ago. It had not been used in a decade. Johnny Harris, or Imani, as he prefers to be called, and I spoke in that witness room. It was for his execution that the old electric chair was moved to Holman Prison and given a new coat of paint.

The prison authorities would give us only thirty minutes at a time to talk and that amount only once a month. But as we began to talk and the yellow chair stared at us from the other room I wondered if there wasn't a reason for limiting interviews to thirty minutes. Having death row inmates interviewed next to the electric chair seems a cruel joke. Limiting the interviews to thirty minutes is probably someone's idea of mercy.

Johnny "Imani" Harris, thirty-two, sits on Alabama's death row convicted of the murder of a prison guard during an uprising at the other prison in Atmore in 1974. At the time of the uprising he was serving five concurrent-life sentences for rape and robbery that he had received in 1970. He maintains that he is innocent of all the charges against him.

He is not alone in that contention. A large group of supporters around the world have set up a defense committee, The Committee to Defend Johnny "Imani" Harris and Stop the Death Penalty, hired lawyers and investigators and have made his case a cause celebre that climaxed when the U.S.S.R. singled out Johnny Harris as a political prisoner and an example of human rights violations in the U.S. This type of support, as well as the exposure his case has received, is, of course, extraordinary. Most death row inmates are faceless people, with little outside support, unknown even in their own states.

In August of 1970 Johnny Harris, living with his family in an all-white neighborhood in Birmingham, was stopped by the police on his way to work, asked if he would cooperate with a line-up downtown and, once downtown, was charged with the rape of a white girl and four robberies. All of those offenses at the time could have been capital cases. Harris did not fit the description given the police by the rape victim but he was taken to trial. His lawyer did not visit or talk to him before the trial and subpoenaed none of the alibi witnesses Harris requested to testify for him. Seeing the unpreparedness of his counsel and the possibility that he could be executed for any of the crimes he says that he took a deal and pleaded guilty, he thought, to the rape charge. He actually pleaded guilty to all five charges and was given five life sentences. This version of Harris' trial was corroborated by his then attorneys in their testimony at a 1979 hearing held to discern their competency in handling the Harris case.

Johnny Harris went to Atmore Prison, the twin to Holman prison, now called officially the G.K. Fountain Correctional center. In 1972 Atmore was the scene of peaceful strikes and demonstrations against prison conditions that were led by a group called Inmates for Action (IFA). The uprising was quelled when the leaders of the IFA were put in segregation. Johnny Harris, who sympathized with the protest, wound up in segregation too when he was charged with attempted escape in 1973. The protesters, isolated in their cells, maintained a unity of sorts and carried on their effort aimed at changing prison conditions that, several years later, U.S. District Judge Frank M. Johnson called, "barbaric, cruel, and unusual" and "unconstitutional."

On January 18, 1974 the inmates on segregation took two guards hostage and asked to see members of the press, clergy, prison administration and legislature. The prison was quickly and violently retaken by a shooting attack on the segregation unit led by Warden Marion Harding. One of the hostages, Luell Barrow, was killed, apparently stabbed by his captors. One of the leaders of the IFA, George "Chicinga" Dobbins, was killed by a shotgun blast and nine stab wounds to the head. Four months later Johnny Harris and three others were indicted for Barrow's murder. Harris was personally prosecuted separately from the others by Attorney General William Baxley. Under an 1862 law that had been used only seven times before, Harris was convicted of first degree murder and, unlike his co-defendants, was given the death penalty. The old law, the only death penalty statute in effect in Alabama at the time of Johnny Harris' trial, provided for the death of a person convicted of a murder while serving a life sentence.

He and the three others eventually convicted of Luell Barrow's murder came to be known as the Atmore-Holman brothers and got a wide range of attention in the South and support for their defense from around the world. The racial and political overtones of the case continue to the present. Two of the Atmore-Holman brothers died in prison and supporters claim the deaths were neither accidents nor suicides as authorities contend. No investigation of those deaths has yet taken place.

Meanwhile Johnny Harris' appeal of his death sentence has been denied. New evidence in the case, however, may be enough to give him a new trial. That new evidence became public early in 1979 but had been available since 1974. Jesse David Jett, a white convict and an eyewitness to the Barrow killing, was listed as an escapee from the Alabama prison system and was picked up in Ohio late in 1974. There he told two attorneys and the FBI that Johnny Harris did not participate in the killing, though he said others of the Atmore-Holman brothers did. He made these statements three months before the trials of the Atmore-Holman brothers. Why this information did not surface until four years later is a mystery that is under investigation by Federal authorities and a Congressional committee. Jett also testified that he had seen prison officials stab George Dobbins to death after they had immobilized Dobbins with a shotgun. The prison officials reported that Dobbins' death had been due to a shotgun wound solely. The coroner's report supports Jett's allegation.

Johnny Harris, the man at the center of this tangle of facts and disputed facts, speaks in a quiet, raspy voice and uses a vocabulary that has a touch of leftist political rhetoric. Clearly his years in prison have made him politically aware. Though his conversation is dotted with wide, quick smiles, his sense of having been abused by the criminal justice system is apparent. His appreciation of his supporters is effusive.

Johnny Harris was handcuffed while we talked and had to go through some minor contortions to light a cigarette. As I changed tapes or picked up my camera he would look through the window at the yellow chair and then, self-consciously, look back at me. He didn't seem unsettled by the chair. Just aware of its presence.

AT AGE TWELVE I was supporting myself on $45 a week. It was the second job I had. When I was ten I got a part-time job in a grocery store and went to school. That was after I flunked one year. I felt like I was flunked for no reason. My grades were up to par. So I began to feel like school was just something I wasn't interested in. I thought the best thing for me to do was to get a part-time job. I went from about 6:30 till about 7:45 in the morning and then after school till about 7:15 or 7:30 at night. Doing all right, you know, for a boy of my age.

This was in Bessemer, Alabama. I mostly grew up in Bessemer. I was born in Choctaw County. My mother was killed when I was three years old and one of my aunts took it upon her to help raise me and my three brothers. And without the help of a husband too. The welfare department was going to put some of us kids in homes because my father couldn't take care of us, but my aunt refused to let them do it. The last time I heard anything about my father was about 1962. He's living somewhere in New Mexico, I think.

The reason we went to Bessemer was because my aunt's only daughter lived in Bessemer and she wanted to be close to her. I understand that, you know. She wanted to be close to her daughter and her daughter wanted to be close to her. But I think I would have liked it better if we had stayed down there in Choctaw County. I just think my whole life would have been different if we had stayed in a less populated area.

My aunt did a beautiful job raising us. I don't fault her for any of the bad luck I've had. It was pretty rough growing up but she would make sure us kids had something to eat, even if it wasn't much, before she would eat herself.

So after I got the job in the grocery store I got a job in a used car lot. I liked working on the cars. Matter of fact I think I was a pretty good shade tree mechanic. That's what I liked about it. The driving wasn't important to me. It was during the second year at the car lot that I decided to quit school and work full time. It was hard for my aunt to get work. So I said, "Look, I might as well go ahead and quit school. Pulling down a paycheck every week will be better on you, more helpful to you."

When I'd get paid off every Friday I'd keep some for myself and give the rest to my aunt. We were on welfare, too. And the only way we were on welfare was to keep the truant lady from finding out that I had quit school. That was a problem. I used to have people in the neighborhood that watched out for her. They would see her coming four or five houses up the street and they would call me. I could drive a car from the lot home, take me a quick bath, put on some clothes and play sick during her visit to keep her from knowing I'd quit school. We couldn't afford to lose that welfare check.

That went on for about a year and then it was in my mind that if I could get this job and work full time I could get a better job and make more. So I started working with gypsies who came to a special place near Bessemer. I was making patio chairs. I was making pretty good money but if it rained we couldn't work. So over all the pay wasn't that good. But I worked hard. When they moved on I had to find another job. I went to a cast iron plant and got a job there. That's when I was making the biggest paycheck I ever made. And I liked the work. It was real dirty. It gets real dirty in a cast iron plant but I liked the work.

I guess it was during the third or fourth year I was out of school that I started drinking a little heavy. And let me see, what was the first thing I went to jail for? I think the first thing I went to jail for was a traffic ticket. And you know I haven't paid that traffic ticket yet. I'm the kind who says, "Don't let a person keep you locked down." I always escaped every time they put me in jail. And that ran the time up til I think it was 478 days. Wait a minute. I did pay that traffic ticket. My brother paid it off in '69. I wrecked my car and I didn't have any driver's license so they took me to jail. The only way he could get me out of the city jail was to pay the old fines. And he payed off the $478. That's what the ticket had run up to.

This all was in Bessemer. The only time I had been in the Birmingham jail was in '69. I broke out of the Bessemer city jail and they had to send me back for breaking out of the city jail. It was a felony so they sent me to the county jail. I had been in the county jail once because of trouble in the neighborhood when we started a peace march. Those were the only two times I was in Birmingham jail. And it just grew from there. I did time in the penitentiary.

When I came home from the penitentiary I met Kate. She had a child and she was separated from her husband. Her step daddy was just like a father figure to me. This put me in a position to see Kate any time I was there. I think most of my concern was directed toward the child. This drew us closer together. We used to sit and talk, take the baby for a walk, go to the store for ice cream and stuff like that. And we just grew closer and closer together. Her husband wouldn't grant her the divorce. If he had granted her the divorce we would have had a church wedding. But he wouldn't do that so she said, "Well, we don't need a divorce. Let's live together." And she and I with her stepfather and her mother decided to buy a house. It was pretty convenient like that. We had two families and one set of bills. So we saved the money, paid the down-payment on a house.

At first we didn't have no trouble with people in the neighborhood. I'm not saying they accepted us with open arms. We were the only black family in this neighborhood. But many people at first seemed to say, "They're not bothering me. Why should I bother them." This is what we were doing. We felt like since we were having no trouble when we first moved in there that that's how people in the neighborhood felt too. But it all changed in about a month, maybe six weeks. The trouble started and it went on all the while we were in the neighborhood. Except for three families everybody else wanted us out. Everybody else did everything they could to run us out. It took so many years to get a down payment on a home that we couldn't just run away like that.

We didn't get a chance to stay in the neighborhood a year before I was picked up on August 11, 1970. I wasn't picked up on any charges. When they stopped the car my mother-in-law was driving. They told her that they were conducting a neighborhood investigation and they wanted to know if I wanted to participate in it. I asked them what was the nature of the investigation and told them I was on my way to work. The man said that they would take me to work once we got through. All there was, he said, was to go downtown and stand in a lineup and then they'd take me to work. That was how they got me downtown. I haven't been told yet I'm under arrest. They didn't even have a warrant.

They charged me with one rape and four robberies. All five of the cases happened in less than a two-mile radius of my neighborhood. I was living on Fayette Street. The drive-in is quite near Fayette. It was less than three blocks from my house. That's where one robbery occurred. If you go down Fayette to Third there is the service station where they say three robberies happened. What they claim is that I robbed one man twice and the third robbery happened on the girl that said she was raped. I'm not saying she wasn't. I'm saying I didn't do it. Now what man would be stupid enough to go and rob places right in the vicinity of the neighborhood he is going to live in? At the service station where he stopped several times to get gas, fix a flat tire and stuff like that? I was known at that service station. The man I worked for was a tree surgeon. That's where he traded and we used to stop there twice a day, he driving and me sitting up in the cab with him. So do I appear that stupid?

I went to the penitentiary with five life sentences. I had been in about three and a half years when the rebellion happened and then I got the death penalty. On the Birmingham case it was a race issue. But on the death penalty case it was Baxley, a political issue because of his ambition to be Governor. He prosecuted me directly. He felt that his direct involvement in prosecuting me would win him the votes.

After that protest took place it took them exactly four months to decide if they wanted to prosecute me or if they were going to have me indicted. But they only decided after getting advice from Baxley's office. Baxley saw this was his chance to prosecute somebody for the death penalty, to bring back the death penalty in the state of Alabama.

From the minute I got the indictment I knew I was in line for the chair. They were hot to use somebody. I was just one of the chosen. There were several other people charged too. But none of them was being charged with a capital offense. They were being tried with murder charges but not in the way I was being tried. They tried me on a law that was at the time 116 years old. At that time in 1975, it was the only death penalty law on the books in the State of Alabama. It said that anyone serving a life sentence that was convicted of a murder shall suffer the death penalty. And I said, "Wait a minute. This means they are going to put the heat on me to take the heat off the system." Because at the same time they were talking about prosecuting me for murder, they weren't saying anything about prosecuting any of the state officials for Chicinga's murder. I believe the folks are out to get me. This death penalty has been real to me right along.

For two years I was on death row by myself. That was probably the most straining time. Being the only one on death row wasn't anything to be proud of. Now there are 40 or 41 on death row and it's still nothing to be proud of. But at the time I felt alone. I couldn't believe it. I knew it was real, but why me? I used to feel if I kept cool this will show the courts the kind of person I really am. Not to deceive anybody—I tried it because it's really me. At the time I was on death row by myself there was more cooperation between the officers and me. I was down there in a single cell, next to the electric chair, the one you're supposed to go to just before you're executed. The segregation cells were upstairs. So finally I made up my mind to see if I could be moved upstairs. When I asked them they told me I could go there if I didn't get into nothing. So I was the only man on death row and I was housed in segregation. That means that when we went out in the exercise yard we got to play basketball together.

*You say you are a target of sorts, you feel like you are. How does that feel?*

Frustrating, of course. Some days you deal with it without being angry, or even upset, or even without dwelling on it for several hours at a time. Then again you can wake up in the middle of the night, even if it's just to use the toilet, and this feeling of being abused is lingering, you can feel it. You say you're tired of this because you know it's in violation of every right you have as a human being. You know that it's even in violation of the rights that the lawmakers put on the books. You know that it is wrong for them to single people out because of their financial status or living area. The man in the cell next to you is in the same situation you're in. It happened to me, it happened to the fella next to me. You can't dwell on it, though. You have to find a non-harmful way to let the tension off. Then you can pretty well bring yourself back down off that frustration trip.

*Does it ever hit you full face that you might die in that electric chair?*

Let me answer that like this. I don't have a whole hell of a lot of confidence in the court system. I accept the fact that the court system is a have and have-not organization and it functions on a have and have-not basis. Now poor people are the only people in penitentiaries. And poor people, and especially Black people are the people being killed by the death penalty law. Sometimes, then, I think that it might be a possibility, I might lose this case. But I won't dwell on it. I still hope for the best.

I understand the system of justice in this country will sacrifice the life of a poor person to put fear in the population of the whole country. Look at John Spenkelink. That's all that was. They sacrificed him to put fear into the population of the state of Florida. I don't believe they had a right to kill him. I don't believe anyone has the right to kill another human being.

Some people say that we should die. They really don't know how the law works. They haven't had this that's happened to me happen to anybody they love. Or to them. But how would they deal with it if confronted with it, if subjected to the same abuse and violation?

Of course the people who send us here realize when they do it that we have feelings, that we have dreams of a happy life with normal living standards. But once we get here members of society think that the judge sent us here because we don't have any respect for the law, we don't have any respect for society, we don't have any feelings, sensitivities, you know. That's lies. People on death row share and feel and exercise those qualities daily. It is only because people on the outside don't know how the law works that they think that way.

But there is another side to this too. I have received only about five percent of my support in this case from my family because my family is still poor. But I have received the rest of my support from strangers, people that sympathize with me because of my situation and because they understand how abusive and corrrupted the law is. These people have really contributed to me being able to deal with this. My strength is not self-developed or self-manufactured. These people have given me a lot. They are my source of strength. I'm not just speaking of finances. They say they can see the fault in the system and they feel they should support us in some kind of way, even if it's only to write letters of encouragement. It's the love and concern and understanding these people show that I appreciate.

*You've gotten a lot of support in your case from people in this country and abroad. Why is that?*

I think it's because they believe I'm innocent just like I know I'm innocent. I'm not the type of person that will take advantage of people or abuse anybody's kindness, friendship or support. If I were guilty of any of these charges I would not let hardworking people out there spend their money for lawyer fees and investigative work. If I were guilty I would always be man enough to admit anything I did and accept punishment for it.

*(At this point a guard opened the door to the room we were in and told us our time was up. Johnny got up and while I was packing up my tape recorder and cameras he looked at the electric chair.)*
*What do you feel when you look at that?*

I don't have any special feelings when I see it. I don't have any intentions of sitting there. No way. There is a possibility that I might lose my case. I just don't feel like I'm going to make it there.

# Elvin Myles

Eighteen months after Elvin Myles was born his father killed his mother in their hometown, Amite, Louisiana, forty-five miles northeast of Baton Rouge. Not only did the murder leave Myles without a mother but, he says again and again, his father's reputation as a murderer branded him, his father's only son, as "the devil" in the small, segregated town. That branding, Myles suspects, shaped the entire course of his life, twenty-seven years riddled with serious crimes, very tough prison sentences, police harassment, little productive work and finally a first-degree murder, robbery conviction on April 25, 1978 that resulted in a sentence of death.

The Louisiana State Prison in Angola, Louisiana, referred to by most people in the state as simply Angola, has been Elvin Myles's home for seven of the past twelve years. A sprawling, antiquated prison farm and maximum security prison on the banks of the Mississippi river five miles below the Mississippi-Louisiana border, Angola, formerly a plantation, looks at times as though it has changed little in the past hundred years. Lines of convicts file out at dawn to chop cotton or cut sugar cane, watched by shotgun-carrying guards on horseback. Myles was first sent to Angola when he was fifteen years old. He did six years on that sentence, a small part of it at a juvenile institution but the majority of it among the most hardened criminals in the state. During that time, he says, he had no contact with anyone outside the prison, not a letter nor a visit from either family or friends.

On release Myles moved to New Orleans to work but soon moved back to Amite. Arrested for a fight with a policeman, he spent thirty months in a parish jail. He says that because of the nature of the charge, striking a police officer, no attorney in the area would take his case and he defended himself. Shortly after his release from this sentence he was arrested for the robbery-murder that put him on death row. He is convicted of killing Lucille Erikson, the aunt of the Amite Police Chief, during the holdup of her convenience store.

In Louisiana people sentenced to death do not go to Angola until their sentence is upheld by the Louisiana Supreme Court. While awaiting the decision of the high court they remain in the parish jail. In August of 1979 there were twelve people in the state of Louisiana under sentence of death but only one of them, Elvin Myles, sat on death row at Angola. A year and two months after he was convicted of Lucille Erikson's murder the Louisiana Supreme Court upheld the conviction.

Of all the death rows I have seen, the one at Angola is certainly the bleakest. A large old building near the front gate of the huge prison farm serves as the maximum security unit. In the back part of this building is a row of cells designated death row. Though there are others in those cells none but Myles is now under an active death sentence.

I interviewed him at his cell. It was painted a flat white with dull gray bars. He had some reading material stuck under his mattress and a drawing he had done on the wall. A cover on the toilet kept the rats from swimming out at night, he said. The cell fronted on a stone walkway that was cracked and unpainted. Along the wall of the hallway were three big, old, black and white televisions blaring out soap operas.

At first Myles said he would not speak to me. He had been told by the guards that I was a television reporter. When I sent a note back to him explaining who I was, he agreed to speak to me, saying later that he had had bad experiences with the press and would not speak to them. I had to stand outside his cell for the interview. I put my tape recorder on the bars and we began to talk. Myles, a somewhat sullen and powerful looking man, seemed to shrink from the tape recorder ever so slightly. After an hour or so of conversation I found that I had to move the tape recorder over closer to him. He had moved out of its range. During the course of the interview I had to do this several times finally ending up with him up against the wall of his cell and my tape recorder on the bars near the wall. It was at this point that we started to talk about the crime for which he was given the death penalty. He had a great deal of trouble saying anything about the crime. The small whirring noise of the tape recorder, just audible through the din of the soap operas, nearly drowned out his words.

He speaks very softly anyway. His speech is mumbled and, to a northerner, thickly accented. His sentences are short and his answers to many questions were abrupt. Through most of the interview he was guarded and suspicious. At times he was downright evasive. But these protective devices seemed to me to come more from a need to avert pain than from guile.

Elvin Myles is not only alone on death row at Angola but, more than anyone else on death row that I talked with, he is alone in the world. In the past twelve years he has had to deal mostly with courts and prison officials, whom he distrusts with a passion, and with fellow prisoners he has never learned to accept as friends. His feelings of persecution have led him to contemplate suicide rather than an execution because he detests the idea of people enjoying his death in the electric chair.

One of the books Myles had in his cell that he said interested him was a book of retold Bible stories. He was thinking about being baptized, he said. In calling back to Louisiana to check some facts months after our interview I found out that he had been baptized by a

Roman Catholic priest in the visiting room near death row on Christmas Eve. He was the only one being baptized and in the small service he had to read responsively from a lectionary. He was handcuffed and shackled so tightly that a guard had to help him turn the pages.

MY DADDY KILLED my mother when I was eighteen months old. My aunt took me then. Took five of my sisters and brothers.

*What happened to your father?*
I think he got a life sentence. Ninety years. He got out. I haven't seen him for a while.

*Did you keep up with him at all when he was in prison?*
We never did get any kind of relationship. We never was tight. Never could get close. Never could get a relationship going.

*Did your aunt have kids of her own?*
She had four. There were ten kids all together. She did domestic work. My uncle was a logger, you know, cut logs and things and brought 'em out of the woods.

*What was it like growing up in Amite?*
I don't like the place. I ran away from there. I went to Michigan.

*How old were you?*
I was about thirteen. Twelve or thirteen years old. I was just hitchhiking. I just ran off. I knew two families in Michigan. I stayed with them while I got a job in a packing company.

*You were only thirteen years old?*
Yeah. I set my age up because, you know, I was kinda big for my age.
When I was in Michigan I met this dude from Detroit. He influenced me to rob. I was about fourteen and he was about thirty or thirty-two. He influenced me to rob stuff. So when I came back here I just had a habit of robbing. I came back and got in some trouble down here. Aggravated burglary, armed robbery. So they sent me over here.

*They sent you over to Angola? How old were you then?*
Fifteen. It was armed robbery. They fixed it so I wouldn't go to a juvenile institution somewhere. They sent me up here. They wanted me to be around all them criminals.

*They wanted you to?*

Yeah. They changed my charge. I didn't know nothing about the law. So they told me everything. You know fifteen years old I didn't know about this stuff. I copped a plea. They tacked sixteen charges on.

*Sixteen charges?*

My lawyer advised me to do that. I didn't know what to do. Like I say I was young, really young. If I had it to do now, I never could do it. But I didn't know anything then.

*What were some of the other charges?*

Mostly burglaries and robberies.

*Had you done any of them?*

I did the one I got busted on. A robbery. That was it. I was in Michigan when the rest of them happened. Attempted rape was the charge they used to get me in the penitentiary. You can't send a juvenile to Angola unless it's a capital charge, semi-capital charge, attempted aggravated rape, first-degree murder, second-degree murder. So they can charge on me.

*Had you done that, the attempted rape?*

No.

*Why do you think they were after you like that?*

I've been trying to figure that out myself. I think my father had a bad name. I guess it never paid for us. My father been over here three or four times for murder. Everybody look at me like I'm a . . . I don't know . . . like I was the devil or something.

*Did your brothers have the same problem?*

No we don't have the same father. We have different fathers. We don't even associate. We're not very close. I have a sister in New Orleans. I'm close with her. I can't communicate with her too much. Stayed away from her too long now. There's a big gap between us. We're in different worlds or something. First time I stayed up here six years and I didn't even get a visit. Didn't write a letter or nothing.

*You were in Angola from the time you were fifteen until you were twenty-one and never got a visit?*

Never got a visit. Never wrote a letter. So there's a big gap between us.

When I first got here they sent me to this little place, De Quincey. It's supposed to be for first offenders and juveniles. At first they had me upstairs here in the control unit because they didn't want me in population. I went to De Quincey over near Texas. I stayed there about ten months and I got in a fight with somebody and they sent me back here. I had made seventeen then and they sent me on the big yard. I was cutting cane, picking cotton. About eleven months I stayed in the field.

I ain't never seen nothing like that. Had to get up about five-thirty, six and go eat breakfast, go get on the thing called hootenanny or something like that and go to the field and get off. They have guard lines set up and you can't step outside the line. Four cornered guard line and you can't step outside the line. You do and they might shoot your leg. They might shoot in the air to warn you. When they had inmate guards they'd shoot you for nothing. They shoot you and they get six months off their time. That's why they got rid of all them inmate guards. They was killing up one another.

It was just a whole lot of work. I don't know, I guess that's where all their money is coming from, the sugar cane, you know.

*Did you ever go to any kind of schooling or anything like that?*

I went to carpentry school, butchering and slaughtering school, refrigeration and air conditioning. I went to mechanic school at De Quincey.

*Did you use any of that when you got out?*

Yeah. I did a little. I had a construction job and I was doing a little carpentry work, you know, repairing and things. But it's hard to stay in school. See they enroll you in school but if you get a write-up or disciplinary report or anything they'll take you out of school and throw you in the field. It's hard not to get a write-up because a free man, he'll harass you, write you up for nothing, the least thing. Especially when picking cotton or cutting cane time comes cause they be waiting for you to do something so they could take you out of school. They didn't want you in school anymore. They want you in the field. So it's hard to stay in school.

I managed to stay in butchering school and carpentry school during the summer. As soon as the winter came they took me out. I never knowed anybody to get a certificate or anything from the school. Just learn a little bit, I guess. I asked the instructor about a certificate. He told me that the reason you don't get a certificate is you never finished the trade. That's what he tells me.

*What kind of people did you meet when you went into Angola at age fifteen?*

There were all kinds. Most of the guys wanted to be cowboys or something. They think they're cowboys.

*What do you mean they wanted to be cowboys?*

They think they're cowboys. They'd be walking around, man, have big old knives on their belt, toting big old knives. They called them guns. They just have a mental problem.

*What did you learn from them?*

I learned that they do all kinds of things. Somebody might learn your name and number. Then they get into it with a free man and the free man write 'em up. He might give your name and number. Then you be going to court and you don't know what you be going to court for. Stuff like that. They be doing all kinds of mischievous things against one another, the majority of them. They have very few be into something constructive.

On the big yard I was the one with the shortest time to go there. Everybody else had two lives, fifteen hundred years, stuff like that. And every day they might be looking around the dormitories and they come out there swinging knives and fighting. I had a couple of fights. They always trying to get me into a fight thinking that I'm about to go home. I didn't want no part of it. Why they kept me around those people when I had so little time I don't know. Once I got stabbed. I believe they was trying to get me stabbed. I goes to the hospital. And they sent me right back to the same dormitory. Twice they did me like that.

*You got out when you were twenty-one?*

Twenty-one.

*What did you do then?*

I got a job on construction. It was in New Orleans. Repairing schools and things that might get burned down. We'd tear it up and replace it. My uncle had an uncle working there and he referred me to it.

*Then what happened?*

The contract ran out or something and we had to sign up for unemployment. But I just never did go back to the job. I went to another job at the Chevrolet company. I drove a wrecker, did odd jobs. I stayed there for a while and then I left New Orleans. I liked New Orleans but there were just too many people, you know. I had to get away from the crowd, back to the country cause I don't like crowds. I didn't do nothing but I got arrested when I got back to Amite. And got out and got arrested again. Got arrested a lot of times but I never went to court or went to trial. They was kidnapping me was what they was doing. Taking me to jail. That's all they was doing. Time I'd get ready to go to court they release me cause they didn't have no case. Kidnap me and put me in jail. Sometimes I'd spend months, weeks in jail. From three days to three months. They even take me to an arraignment one time. Once they set no bond on me to keep me in jail, saying I'm on parole. Anything just to hold me in jail. I couldn't figure out why. I still don't know why. Must be my father or something. Gotta be something out of the past.

*What was your neighborhood like?*

Mostly poor people. Segregated mostly. I lived with my uncle. Helped him work a little bit on his log truck and things, you know.

I got a job in the saw mill til they started harassing me. When they found out I was in town they started harassing me, watching me. I'd be in town and they'd grab me and shake me down. They'd see me with a bag and they'd take the bag and look all in it. Anything, just anything to harass me. This went on the whole while I was out. I didn't have much fun out there. It was like a war or something like that. That's what it was. Like I was in Vietnam or something.

One day I got tired of being harassed. Policeman came to me and we got in a fight. I hit him with my hand and cut his eye open. They said I was a boxer or something. The dude weigh 300 pounds and I weighed 175 pounds. I did it because he kicked me. I just went berserk. Took his pistol too. And some more policemen came and tried to get me off him. About sixteen of them. They got me in the car and brought me there and put about sixteen charges on me of assault and battery and resisting arrest and all kinds of charges. All the charges were six month charges. Took me to trial. Gave me a six man jury and everything. They tried me on all sixteen charges. I fought the case. I think I got thirty-two months out of the deal.

*Did you have a court-appointed lawyer or a public defender?*

None of those lawyers from around there would take my case. Because all my charges were for hitting a police officer. Nobody around there would take it.

*So who took your case?*

Nobody.

*You had no lawyer?*
Just myself.

*Did you have to do the whole time?*
I did the thirty months and I got out and I went back to New Orleans. I didn't even slow up in Amite. About a month later I came back and I got a job with that same saw mill. You could get a job there anytime because people are always quitting. So I got a job at the saw mill.

I had made some friends, a lot of friends. I started liking the place a little bit. Before then I couldn't get around the police officer in my house, that's all. I mean the place is not bad. But some of the people, man. . . . To me it was hell. But still I went back there.

About two months after I went back I got busted on this charge. The DA told me he was going to get me on something. DA Joe Simpson. He had promised me something. See I wrote him a letter one time and talked to him pretty bad, you know, about not bringing me to trial soon enough, bringing me to court on time. He laughed when he promised to get me.

*What was the charge?*
Armed robbery and murder.

*What happened?*
I don't know. I was strung out on drugs and, I don't know, I got pretty high, all kinds of high. I don't even too much remember about the thing. The day the charge took place I can't even give an account for it, where I was or nothing, who I was with. I thought I knew who I was with but they wouldn't even come to court to testify, say they didn't want to get involved. So I don't even know who I was with. I was so messed up. So I didn't have no alibi.

*When were you picked up?*
Supposed to be the day after the crime, the morning after. I was picked up at a motel. I was asleep and they kicked the door down.

*Did you have a lawyer for the trial?*
Um, no.

*You mean you went to trial without a lawyer?*
I had a lawyer but he was working against me. He was a public defender. He was doing all kinds of things that he wasn't

supposed to be doing. He told somebody that I was paying somebody to kill him. I didn't even have money to get myself a lawyer. Man, it was unbelievable what they was doing. There's a conspiracy against me, that's all.

*What do you do during the day?*
Read a little bit, pace the floor, walk up and down, pace the floor and watch TV there. Watch the news. That's about all I watch. That's all there is. I get an hour out in the walkway there and a shower.

I write letters. I haven't been doing too much because they don't want to give stamps in the mail any more. If I get a money order out of the streets it takes three weeks for it to get in my account and another two weeks before you get your stamps and about six weeks before you can put some money in the store.

*Is it hard to write people on the outside?*
It's not hard to write. There's just nothing to talk about. Nothing new, same thing every day.

*How long have you been here?*
Since January. Almost seven months.

*Have you had any visitors?*
No. I have talked to the news some. But not anymore. That's why I said I wouldn't talk to you at first. They told me you was a TV man. I don't talk to TV people because they get on the TV, they exaggerate. If I tell them one thing, they get on the TV and say another thing. So I don't talk to them.

But I haven't had a regular visit in six months. To have a visit you have to have people fill out some papers, a lot of papers. That takes about six weeks. Then they have to send their names to the FBI file and all that shit. The reason they denied my sister is because she forgot to sign the paper to let them search her. She could have done that over here. So it will be after August when she can come.

*Do you have a wife or children?*
I had a common law wife.

*Does she come and visit you?*
No. I stopped writing her when I got sentenced. Seemed like it didn't make sense to be writing. I had too much time, you know. I told her to find somebody else. I still feel like that.

*Do you go out on the yard by yourself or with other inmates?*

I'm not allowed to even get in contact with nobody. Can't even be in the hall at the same time with nobody. Can't get on the yard together with no man. I have to do everything by myself.

*Do you talk to the people in the cells next to you?*

They want me to talk to them but they ain't talking about nothing. Talk to 'em sometimes.

*Do you talk to the guards?*

They trick you. See I know their ways. They like to play. They play with dudes. Dude say something they don't like they might talk about the dude's momma or something. Dude say something he don't like he'll write out a report and send him to the hole for ten days. They got something to say, I'll listen. But I don't play or anything.

*What's the hole like?*

Not much worse than this! They got a cell with no mattress. You have to sleep on the floor. For ten days. They give you a mattress about eight o'clock and take it about three in the morning. I been up there once. Got in an argument with a free man. When they write you up they don't put down what really happened. They exaggerate. And there it is—your word against a free man's word. So that's why I stopped talking to 'em. They practice at harassing people.

*So you don't talk to anybody?*

Sometimes I go play cards on the hall after I take my shower. I play dominoes. We talk but what I mean is what we talk about ain't hitting on nothing. You know it's just talk.

*I noticed that you didn't eat lunch. Why is that?*

I don't think I need it. When I eat too much I can't think. I lay down and go to sleep. If I don't eat I can think better. I get uncomfortable if I eat too much.

Also I don't eat too much because when I was in the jail there was something in the food that made me go on a trip. I thought I was supernatural or something. I tried to walk through the bars. And I wouldn't talk to nobody. I think they had put something in the food. I was laying down and I was seeing all kinds of things. At one time I thought I walked through the bars. I made it out but I came back in and walked back through 'em.

I was high, talking about I wanted to die. All kind of things, you know. I was hearing things and I was seeing things. Magical things. I was seeing . . . I ain't never seen my momma so I was seeing my momma and all kinds of things. I was seeing graveyards. I was seeing myself sitting on top of a grave, seeing babies being born, seeing the sheriff getting his leg cut off. It was a trip. Seemed like I was in pain. Didn't scare me but it lasted too long. The trip lasted too long. Seemed too real.

*This is a pretty old cell block. What's it like here?*

They're supposed to be building a new building for death row. I think this building is condemned. Been condemned since the early sixties. See them water spouts. When it rains water be in every cell down the line. The toilet leaks. Rats come up through the toilet and jump on the floor at night. That's why that cover's on it. They got rats that are big and fast. Can't kill 'em. Guy next to me killed a couple. They're too quick for me.

*Were you expecting a death sentence at your trial?*

Yeah, I was expecting it. The DA told me the time he saw me, you know, when they first brought me out, when he first saw me, that he was going to give me the electric chair. And the whole jury was from Amite.

The death sentence is so one-sided, you know. It makes you kind of mad sometimes.

*How is it one-sided?*

You see murder is murder. If they're going to sentence me to die then what about others who murder. Another guy went to trial in Amite. He shot a fifteen year old boy in the head with a .357 magnum. Died on the spot. He didn't get the electric chair. Like I say it's one-sided. That's why I don't like to think about it. It makes me disgusted.

*How did you feel when you were given a death sentence?*

I felt like I was floating somewhere. I felt high, like I got high. You know, I didn't believe it. It didn't sound real. Like I was dreaming sort of, that's all.

*Has it hit you that you might die in the electric chair?*

It hit me but I don't got to it, frankly. Because I know if I die in the electric chair they'll watch it, you know. I done got to the point where I been worrying and worrying and worrying and I can't worry no more.

Every now and then I think about it but I can't picture myself walking to no electric chair. You know I've made up my mind that I would try to kill myself before I go in the electric chair. I don't believe I give them the opportunity to sit back and laugh and talk about it, how he did this and that . . . I think I'd rather take my ownself out. They come in and find me dead with a note or something like that. I think that's probably what I'll do. I thought about it a lot and I still come up with . . . you know I can't picture myself walking all the way down to an electric chair, sitting down and . . .

I ain't afraid to die but I don't want to die in no electric chair. I know I got to die one day. I don't know how I'm going to die yet but I can't think of the chair.

It's not the chair itself. It'd be over so quick I guess it don't hurt. It's not the electric chair. Just the people that are pushing the electric chair, pushing the death penalty. I wouldn't like to give them the pleasure of seeing me in the electric chair. I feel like I'd be taking something away from them. People that is pushing this, they want this, they want to see this. I'll be taking a thrill from them by taking myself out. They're going to say something on it like, "We didn't get a chance to get him. He took hisself out." Something like that. That's the way I think anyway. There are a lot of people who like to see these kinds of things. I'd be taking something from them.

*How do you feel about the people who want to have that thrill?*

I don't know. There's something the matter with them. They got a problem. They ain't doing nothing but digging their own graves, because anyday they could fall in the same position and there it is. Anybody could get a murder charge like that unintentionally or anything. You could get a murder charge and be innocent, have nothing to do with it. People that are pushing the death penalty are really sick, blind.

*What do you mean blind?*

They don't know what they're doing is what I mean. They are going to have children and grandchildren and you know how wild this generation is. Think how wild the children will be, you understand. They going to have a lot of children down in that chair, in those gas chambers, in front of those firing squads. And they going to be the cause of it. Whoever is pushing the death penalty.

*They probably don't think their kids can ever be that kind of person.*

Nobody think their children do wrong. Nobody ever thinks that their child will grow up and be in prison, go to prison, be sentenced to die.

*If you get your death sentence overturned you'll probably spend the rest of your life behind bars. Do you hope for that?*

I'd rather have a life sentence, I guess. You got a chance with a life sentence. Anything might happen. When you're dead, you're dead.

# Keith Berry

Zelma Shanks returned home from work in the gathering dark of a winter evening, February 9, 1978. The farm she and her husband John owned was in a secluded rural area near Fall Branch, Tennessee, in the eastern part of the state. She drove her car into the garage attached to the house and turned off the headlights. As she climbed out of the car two men grabbed her, dragged her to a top floor bedroom in the house and beat her unconscious. The two fled in her car. Zelma Shanks, sixty-six, was near death from the beating. Her husband, seventy-four at the time, lay dead two floors below her, brutally beaten.

Ten weeks after the murder-beating the police arrested Russell Keith Berry, twenty-six, for the crime. Keith Berry, as he is known, was, then, the Shanks' son-in-law. The District Attorney General said the motive for the crime was Berry's supposed desire to inherit the Shanks' farm, valued at $100,000.

It took Mrs. Shanks months to fully recover from her beating. At her son-in-law's trial, however, her memory and speech had returned. She had seen her attackers, she said, and could identify them "until the day I die . . . No, Keith Berry wasn't either one of them."

The state presented circumstantial evidence to support its theory that Keith Berry had driven the 300 miles from Nashville to Fall Branch to commit the crime. There he supposedly met an accomplice who drove him to the Shanks', met him in a shopping center parking lot after the crime, and then drove him to a nearby airport where Berry flew back to Nashville. The state also presented a hammer found in Berry's car as the murder weapon.

Keith Berry was convicted of the murder of his father-in-law and was sentenced to die in Tennessee's electric chair. Because of Mrs. Shanks' testimony he was not even indicted for her beating.

The case is, in short, unresolved and confusing. Keith Berry has claimed from the beginning that he is innocent of the charges against him. He and his lawyer are hoping that the Tennessee Supreme Court will grant him a new trial, partly on the grounds that the alleged murder weapon, the hammer from Berry's car, was found in an illegal search.

Keith Berry's arrest and conviction for his father-in-law's death were his first ever. The son of a truck driver and a housewife and the oldest of three brothers, Berry was born and raised in Johnson City, Tennessee. Upon graduation from high school in 1970 he worked construction and attended night classes at a local college. About to be drafted, he volunteered for the Army in 1971 and was sent to Vietnam to do clean-up operations in bombed-out areas of Cambodia. Though not many of his unit were killed he describes his tour of duty as a "rough time." After the service he returned to college in Johnson City and went full time, studying accounting. Within a year or so he began working for a trucking concern and eventually quit school to work full time. While at school he met a nursing student, Robin Shanks. When she moved to Nashville to do graduate work in nursing, he followed and they were married some six months before he was arrested.

Keith Berry is a shy, quiet, enigmatic man. Our conversation began very slowly and only after hours of talk did he begin to expand on his answers to my questions. Even then he was guarded and quite suspicious of me. But for the most part the story Berry told me checked out with the facts of the case as I could gather them later. At one point, however, he spoke to me about his parents in the present tense. I was not aware at the time that they had died in a murder-suicide three years before.

Keith Berry is a pleasant person to meet. In the noise and clutter of the Tennessee death row he seems to have carved out a calm niche for himself. He is articulate and measured in everything he says. His thoughts, for the most part, are considered and deliberate. When I raised questions about his guilt or innocence, the fairness of his trial and the problem of the death penalty in such a thorny case, he was typically nonplussed. He said that he did not expect to be believed right off and that the burden of proof of his innocence was his. He knows that he has an uphill fight. He wears his disillusionment with the proceedings in his case, with the press and law enforcement officers who investigated him, like a torn shirt.

In the months I have had to think about the case I find that my detective juices always start pumping as soon as I return to it. I want to unravel all the tangled bits of evidence and make sense of them. I could not do that but I was reminded of a fictional corollary that also will not go away. In Dashiell Hammett's *Thin Man,* Nick Charles comes to the end of a murder mystery and is pretty sure he has his man. The ever-inquisitive Nora begins to ask questions about the case:

> "Just one," Nora said. "But this is just a theory, isn't it?"
> "Call it any name you like. It's good enough for me."
> "But I thought everybody was supposed to be considered innocent until they were proved guilty and if there was any reasonable doubt they—"
> "That's for juries not detectives. You find the guy you think did the murder and you slam him in the can and let everybody know you think he's guilty and put his picture all over news-

papers, and the District Attorney builds up the best theory
he can on what information you've got and meanwhile you pick
up additional details here and there, and people who recognize
his picture in the paper—as well as people who'd think he was
innocent if you hadn't arrested him—come in and tell you things
about him and presently you've got him sitting on the electric
chair . . ."

"But that seems so loose."*

Keith Berry has met the Nick Charleses, has been slammed in the
can and may one day be sitting on the electric chair. He says that no
matter what the outcome of his case he will not be executed; he will
take his own life. Over all the questions about his case hangs the
central one we are concerned with here, the sentence of death. Keith
Berry, as you will see, is surprisingly philosophical on that point. Life
is unfair, he says. Indeed, but I tend to side with Nora.

MY FATHER-IN-LAW WAS murdered on February 9th, 1978. My
mother-in-law was beaten up pretty badly at the same time at
their home. I think it happened on a Thursday afternoon after
she got off work around five-thirty. She was unconscious so
nobody knew about it until the next day.

She was probably unconscious for twenty-four hours at
least when somebody happened to come along, a neighbor or
something, and discovered this and they took her to the hospital.
They first thought she was dead. The deputy, he just looked at
her and thought she was dead. My wife and I had started back
home from Nashville and we just happened to call to tell them
we were going to be late getting there. I called and the sheriff
answered the phone. He told me that they had taken her to the
hospital in Knoxville. So we stopped there. She stayed in
the hospital about three weeks. She had a head injury and
damaged optic nerve to one of her eyes. The part of her brain for
speech and memory was damaged. At first she could hardly talk.
She couldn't really remember what happened at first, just
remembered getting home from work. But she got better and
better. Then she started remembering things. But this was not
until after I was arrested. The police had started asking
questions around and they eventually arrested me about ten
weeks later.

*What was their evidence? Did someone say they saw you there?*
No, nobody saw me there or anything like that. They said they

---

* Dashiell Hammett, *The Thin Man* (New York: Alfred A. Knopf, Inc., 1972), p. 174.

saw a car that resembled mine there, that was it. As far as the evidence they had when they arrested me, that was about it. Just general suspicion, I think.

*Had you and your in-laws been having problems?*
Oh no, we got along real well.

*They didn't have any problems with you two living together before you were married?*
Well, see, they didn't know about that, so that wasn't a problem. I think they suspected it but they didn't say anything. Since we were married later I don't guess it really bothered them that much. No, we got along very well.

I did not get along well with the guy from the Tennessee Bureau of Criminal Investigation, the guy that arrested me. We had pretty hard feelings for one another even before I was arrested. I objected to his general attitude about things. That was the first time I was ever arrested. I didn't know what was going on.

*You'd never had any run-ins with the law before that arrest?*
None. This was the first time. They brought me from Nashville to Greeneville and put me in jail. That's the first time I was ever in jail. It's a shocking experience, I'll tell you. It disorients you completely. The city jail in Greeneville, where they put me is a relatively new jail, it's a pretty clean jail. But still I walked into those bleak surroundings and I was shocked. They take your freedom and lock you up and put you in this cage, really, is what it amounts to. It made me very angry. I guess it would anybody. That's probably a normal reaction.

So they had this undercover agent in the cell at the time they put me in there. He started asking me all these questions about the case. I told him I didn't have anything to do with it and when it came to trial he testified. But instead of using my words he took everything out of context. He made me sound like I knew something about what happened. But he didn't say I did it or even that I said I did it. Just made me sound like I knew something about it. That's the way he told it. It was real damaging to me, very damaging.

*Did you ever say something to him like you think you know who did it?*
No, no. What he said would be like, "What have they got?" And I said, "I don't really know what they've got. Evidently they've got something or I wouldn't be here." I was telling him

as much as I knew. For example I told him about the condition of the house after the murder. I had seen it. But when he told it he made it sound as if I was there. And he asked me, "Have they got your fingerprints?" And I said, "Well, my fingerprints might be in the car because I've driven the car." They stole my mother-in-law's car after the murder. And the way he told it in court it made me sound guilty.

I had already retained this lawyer to represent me before I was arrested because they were putting pressure on us. My mother-in-law too, really harassing her constantly. She wasn't really in any physical condition to be put through that at the time. I had had some classes under this lawyer while I was in school. I knew him before. He was a pretty good lawyer.

While I was in jail my mother-in-law and wife came back and testified at the bond hearing that it wasn't me that attacked her. A little while after they arrested me she began to recover her memory. She was remembering more and more and her speech was getting better. She said she saw two men when she got out of the car. The house had a drive-in garage attached to it. They live in a real secluded area and there have been burglaries out there. As a matter of fact there's been one in her house since I've been in jail. And there was one two or three months before this happened. Somebody broke in, messed up the whole house and stole my father-in-law's pistol.

She said she saw two men and they came out of the basement into the garage and attacked her and knocked her unconscious. She said she could identify who she saw. And before they arrested me they had two composite drawings. I didn't see those drawings. My wife did and some other people did. I don't know what they looked like. Plus they said they had a thumbprint from the rearview mirror in her car which they couldn't identify. That didn't come up in court. Anything that would throw doubt off me didn't come up in court, and my lawyer for some reason didn't bring it up.

*They must have had some evidence. What was their evidence?*
The main piece of evidence at the trial that really convicted me was a hammer they got in my car they said was the murder weapon. They took it to the crime lab here in Nashville and did a blood analysis on it and it came back negative, no blood. I don't know how this works. I don't know if you can remove blood from something like that or not, whether it embeds itself on that metal or what. But anyway it came back negative. So then some guy takes it to the medical examiner, the one that performed the autopsy on my father-in-law and he comes up

with a microscopic bit of evidence. He says there's a small piece of tissue and in that tissue is muscle fiber, hair and bone fragments. He said it was a real small bit but he said it was obvious and he said it was visible to the naked eye. You just have to look at it to see it. That's what convicted me. He said the hammer was the murder weapon. That's what got me here.

*You even smile about it.*
Well this man was either lying or was grossly incompetent. I don't see how he could be that incompetent. If somebody invents something on you because they think you're guilty but they can't prove you're guilty, that's just completely crazy. I think that's what this guy did. It's gonna be hard to prove but I hope I can prove it. See I didn't bring anything to court.

*The hammer was in court?*
Yeah, the hammer was, but it didn't have anything on it. He said it had been removed, and during his examination had been so dissected that there's nothing left, no evidence left except my hammer and his word that it was on the hammer. What me and my attorney are really concerned about is the process in which they conduct the blood analysis. I don't know what that involves and neither does he. But they came up with no blood. If there's gonna be anything on the hammer surely blood would be included.

My lawyer wasn't really prepared for this because we got the report back from the lab earlier but we didn't get this medical examiner's report until about a week before the trial, less than a week before the trial. So we didn't think the hammer was an issue, and that was what really got me convicted. We tried to call another medical examiner in order to have him examine this other doctor's findings. He came down but he said there was nothing he could do. He just had this guy's report to read. He couldn't contradict that.

*How long did the trial last?*
The trial itself lasted four days.

*And why did you get the death penalty?*
Aggravated circumstances. They said it was a heinous, brutal murder. They had to find aggravating circumstances and this is what they came up with. I had three mitigating circumstances which they said didn't outweigh the aggravating circumstances: my age, no prior arrest and something else, I don't remember what the other one was. But really, once you get a jury that

favors capital punishment and they convict you of a capital crime, I guess it's hard to get anything less than that. I didn't expect to. I expected the death penalty from that jury. Because of the pre-trial publicity I expected to be convicted before I walked in the courtroom.

*Did they have a motive?*

Inheritance, supposedly. They said that I wanted them dead for their money. They weren't rich or anything but they had a lot of property.

*And you were unemployed at the time, right?*

Well, no, not really. I don't want to talk about what I was doing because it was illegal. Well, really, I was selling some drugs and they know about that, it's in the court record. That made me sound like a bad person.

*Were you using drugs pretty heavily yourself?*

No, I wasn't using them at all. I was just more or less taking them to other people. That was pretty harmful.

*Once you got the death penalty, how did you deal with that?*

For several reasons I didn't think about the death penalty. I was just too upset over being convicted to begin with. And faced with life imprisonment at the least, that's something that's pretty hard to handle. It's really hard. I was in a state of shock for about a month. And for about six months I was at Brushy Mountain Prison waiting for a motion for a new trial. I didn't do anything while I was there. I just thought the whole time I was there, all sorts of things running through my head. That was the hardest time I've ever had. It was real hard to go through. I guess what kept me going was I knew that these people had lied about me and that's why I was here. I was hopeful that maybe I could bring it all out some day.

*Was there suspicion on your wife's part that you might be guilty?*

No, no. My wife was very upset because she didn't know I was dealing drugs. So was my mother-in-law. But neither one of them think I'm guilty of murder. My wife testified for me. She testified that I was here in Nashville a little more than thirty minutes after the murder occurred.

*How far away was it?*

Well, it's about 300 miles, you know. So they both know that

I'm not the one who did it. But, like I said, they were upset about the drugs. But the only support I can get from anyone right now is moral support.

*Does your wife come to visit often?*

When I was up there in Greeneville in prison she came every day. Nobody comes down here often, though. It's a long ride. You only get two hours to visit when you do come. I don't expect them to come. And I don't have that much to talk about when they come because there's nothing that goes on here, just the same old routine, day in and day out.

*How has your relationship with your wife been?*

Since I've been convicted? Strained. To be honest, if I was to get out tomorrow I probably would never live with her again. Not because of anything she might have done or anything like that. Just because I don't think I could live the type of life that she would expect me to live.

*What do you mean by that?*

It affects you being in here. It changes your outlook on a lot of different things. The court system for one thing, justice in this country. You know, after you're treated like an animal for so long you're going to start acting like an animal. It's hard, really hard. If I do get out of here, I'll probably have little regard for anybody other than myself. But then again sometimes I think I'd like to do things to help people, society in general.

*It sounds like your wife wants to do the same thing through her nursing.*

Yeah, she does. I think I sort of disappointed her in doing what I was doing before I was arrested. She knew . . . we had smoked a lot of marijuana, partied a lot. It's not that she was opposed to it but she didn't want me involved in that way. She thought I was working somewhere else. The fact that I lied to her is what it is. There wouldn't be anything left for us I don't think. It bothers her but it doesn't bother me that much. I have to start a whole new life if I ever do get out of here.

*You keep saying "if" you get out of here.*

Well, I'm not gonna say I'm gonna get out because I have to face this realistically. A lot of people back there on death row think they're gonna get out. I'll tell you right now, most of them aren't gonna get out. Very few of them have a chance to get out. And if you don't face it realistically, you're only fooling yourself. I have a good case for appeal but that doesn't mean I will get out. That doesn't mean I will get a new trial. If I get a new trial that doesn't mean I will be acquitted. I think one man back there has a pretty good shot at being free again. He might have a better chance than I do. As far as the rest of them, I don't think they have a chance to be free again; they won't get acquitted. I don't believe most of them will get a new trial.

*If I knew I was innocent and was given the death penalty I think I'd be very bitter about it. How come you're not?*

Well, everybody on death row's gonna say they're innocent, or most of them anyway. Me saying I'm innocent doesn't mean anything. I know I'm gonna have to prove my innocence. Talk's cheap. It's just a failure in our whole system when that happens, when I have to prove my innocence. Before I was arrested I even had a desire at one time to be a law enforcement officer. I had no idea that they would lie in court to get you convicted. Some of them will go to any means to get a conviction. It helps them in their job, promotion-wise or whatever. I was just completely fooled. I just didn't know how things worked, but now I do. Being cynical isn't going to help me. I try to look at things the way they are. A lot of things in this life are unfair, a lot of things. Nobody said life was supposed to be fair.

*But they are going to execute you.*

Oh, I think of that sometimes, sure. Well, yeah, I have thought about myself in there. I don't think that it'll ever get to that point, but I can't be sure.

*When you can't be sure, when you stare it down, how does that feel?*

I would never go back there. I would commit suicide. If it came down to it, that's what I'd do. There's no way I could face telling somebody, "Take me there and kill me." I would rather kill myself than give them the business, to be honest with you. I think a lot of people feel the same way, though most people don't do it.

*Most people aren't allowed to do it.*

You can't stop a man from killing himself. How are you going to stop that? You'd have to strip him naked. As long as you've got something to hang yourself with you can kill yourself. It's a simple thing to do. It's something that I don't like to think about, but faced with death, I probably would.

*There's always the chance for a stay of execution.*

Well, that's a possibility. But if it got down to that, I would figure I wouldn't have a chance of being free anyway. I'd be faced with a life sentence. I don't know how long you'd have to do on a life, thirty years, probably. Your life's ruined after that. I don't know why they call death capital punishment. They might be doing you a favor. I think I'd rather face the prospect of death than what I know here. This is a hard time, it really is.

Of course I have a prejudiced opinion but there really isn't any purpose served by the death penalty. A deterrent? In Tennessee, capital crime is first-degree murder. First-degree murder has to include premeditation and if somebody thinks out a way to murder somebody, they usually don't even think about being caught. So how's the death penalty gonna be a deterrent? They don't think about the consequences cause they're planning on getting away. Not too many people premeditate getting caught.

*Are you getting used to being in prison, to prison life?*

Life in here is not really life at all. People survive in here because of instinct, I guess. I'm sure if I was off death row, out in population, I'd think about escape. See, there's no hope for it in here. If I was out there, that's all that would be on my mind, getting out. Hopefully, legally. If not legally, I would try to escape. I don't intend to spend my life here.

# J. D. Gleaton

J. D. Gleaton's story is a simple one with a large twist in the middle.

Born thirty-one years ago in Lexington County, South Carolina, Gleaton left school before he had finished the sixth grade to work on a farm and help support his large family. Early in his teens he went south to Florida and began working in the fields there chopping cotton, carrying watermelons and doing any other field work he could find. He worked for a while in New York State as a migrant laborer but soon returned to Florida.

Late in his teens, he found work in a restaurant and eventually became a chef for a large cafeteria chain. It was a big step up for him, a good way out of the field work that he disliked. While in Florida he was arrested for tampering with a phone, and sentenced to three years, but he did only one year before he was paroled. About half of his time in prison, he says, was done on a road gang.

After his year in prison, he lived with a woman he had met who eventually began to work at his restaurant. She became his common law wife and they have two daughters by the marriage. In 1975 they separated and Gleaton moved back to his family home in South Carolina.

On July 12, 1977, Ralph Stoudemire, a filling-station owner in Lexington County was shot and killed during a robbery of his station. A day later the police arrested Gleaton and his brother Larry, then twenty-two, for the murder. They had been driving in Larry's car, one that matched the description of a car seen at the Stoudemire filling-station just before the robbery-murder.

Gleaton and his brother were held without a lawyer or an arraignment for twenty-seven hours and were questioned for most of that time by several police officers. Then near the end of the twenty-seven hours they were visited by another police officer. Shortly after he arrived the Gleatons signed confessions to the Stoudemire murder and were immediately taken to a magistrate.

There had been no witnesses to the killing, only a description of a suspicious car with two black men in it. When Gleaton and his brother were arrested there were four men in their car. Only the Gleatons were arrested. No weapon was found in the car and no money was ever recovered. The Gleatons have never directly been placed at the scene of the crime by anyone. Their confessions convicted them of first-degree murder and robbery and they were sent to death row at the Central Correctional Institution in Columbia.

J. D. and Larry Gleaton now contend that they had nothing to do with the crime, and were coerced into signing confessions. Their lawyer says that even he is not certain how that coercion happened but that their constitutional rights to counsel were violated and the confessions were exacted while that violation was in progress. J. D. Gleaton would say nothing to me about the confession.

We spoke in a cage in the prison's maximum security visiting room. Gleaton had not been aware I was coming and came out a bit disheveled. He is a very polite, quiet man with a quick smile that completely changes what may at first appear to be a threatening look. He is so soft-spoken that at times I could barely hear him. He was open about everything but his confession, about which he referred me to his lawyer, and he was candid about his own lack of education and sophistication.

You would expect that someone who says he had been coerced into signing a confession that may eventually bring his own death would be angry and bitter, and would take every opportunity to lash out at those who put him on death row. I certainly thought so. But J. D. Gleaton would not play that role. He told me that his fate was in God's hands and that he had complete faith that whatever was done to him would be God's will. J. D. did not care whether I believed this or not. In fact I think he expected that I wouldn't. He went on to say that he couldn't be certain why God would execute him for a crime he didn't commit, but was willing to accept his fate whatever it might be.

J. D. Gleaton is by his own admission barely literate. He says that the courtroom vocabulary was far beyond his grasp. He also mentions that when he was first arrested he spent much of the time sleeping. He says that his wife's decision to, in effect, divorce him is the only thing that has "got to" him in a long while, ever since he "knew" himself. He is certainly the most passive person I met during my travels on death row. While it appeared that he was undisturbed by his sentence because of confidence rather than nonchalance, I couldn't help but feel that the major components of that confidence were a naivete about the gravity of his situation and a numbing faith that did not allow for human freedom or error in the divine order.

I will not speculate here on the reasons he and his brother signed a confession to something they now say they didn't do. Those reasons run a gamut from actual guilt to flagrant misconduct by law enforcement agents. They are the twist in J. D. Gleaton's story; not knowing those reasons leaves the central, yawning question of his case unanswered for now. But I didn't meet Gleaton in order to retry his case. I went to meet someone sentenced to die. I met someone hardly able to comprehend his sentence, someone whose life clearly illustrates how some in our society slip through the cracks in our criminal justice system and end up on death row.

I WISH A million times I just went on and finished school. I mean if it had been up to me I would have. But it wasn't up to me. I have trouble with spelling words and knowing the meaning of some words. Even by looking in the dictionary I still have trouble. I don't know anything about the law that much and when they are up there speaking those big words, I don't even know what they are saying. Just a few things I know that I can recognize what they're saying.

*So in the trial it was pretty much beyond you what was happening?*
Right.

*But when you were convicted you knew you had the death penalty. How did that feel?*
It got next to me, you know. I started thinking, "Well, they'll electrocute me, right?" And I read the Bible. I believe in God and so I started thinking about that. Whatever comes now I think God may have a part of it. So I just put my mind and soul into God's hands. Whatever happens God will have a part of it.

*Do you think God would have a part of executing you for something you didn't do?*
If it came down to that I think he would. I think so.

*Why do you think that would be?*
Because he works things in strange ways. He could be working that in for a reason.

*What would the reason be?*
I wouldn't know. I wouldn't know. I believe in God and if anything happens to me, I do believe he will have a part of it. But then again I get to thinking on another turn that the devil is working on the other side. Like it's the devil working on the people that execute me. And the devil can be just as strong as God. I really don't know.

*Why doesn't that make you angry?*
One reason is, like I said, I believe in God, right? Just like I said, he works things in strange ways, OK? It could be his act to place me here. For what reason I don't know. Maybe I was going in the wrong way. Maybe I was going in the direction where I would have eventually ended up on death row. And by somebody else doing this God had it fixed so I could be put here to realize

what the outcome may be. Knowing that I am a good guy but I was going the wrong way, He had sent me here to think, to see that I was going the wrong way. That's the reason that I feel I'll be out of here one day, just because of that.

*You said you wish you had finished school. When did you drop out?*

I quit school in the sixth grade. I was working on the farm and I had to quit school to work, to help with the family and all. My grandmother, well, she said we had to work and help the family. We had a big family. I didn't drop out because I didn't want to go to school. I dropped out to work on the farm.

*What kind of farming was it?*

Picking cotton and chopping cotton, pulling corn and stuff like that. And I never did get to working with a tractor or anything. Only thing I did was chop cotton, pick cotton, pull corn, lug watermelons and stuff like that. And that was pretty hard. I did a little bit of that in Florida also. I went to Florida to start picking fruits. I left there and I went to New York. They call it the tramp bus or something. I went to New York to pick cherries and apples and stuff like that. I left up there for myself. Bought me a car while I was up there. I left New York in '63 and drove it all the way by myself back from New York to Florida. Didn't have any trouble at all. That's when I ended up in Leesburg, Florida. That's when I started washing dishes and then cooking. After I got out of picking fruits that's the only job I ever had was cooking.

When I got to learn how to cook, well, I liked that. If you like something it's not hard on you. So I liked that. I went from fry cook all the way up to chef cook. When I came back to South Carolina in '75 I got a job as a vegetable cook. I told them all I needed to know was their set-up because I knew how to cook. In less than four weeks I was made chef cook.

*You came up from Florida in '75. Do you have any family down there?*

A common law wife and two kids. We lived together for nine years, common law.

*Do you still keep in touch with her?*

Yes I called her yesterday. My youngest girl is eight. She'll be nine December the 20th. My oldest one is eleven. She'll be twelve October the 11th. I met my wife when the cafeteria I was working for transferred me to Coco, Florida. About a month after I met her, she started working at the cafeteria with me.

*Why did you come back to South Carolina?*
Well my wife and I had a misunderstanding. I left for a while and came home. I lived with my mother. If I'd stayed in Florida a couple of days longer our misunderstanding would have been all over. We could have straightened it out. I wanted to come home anyway for a while. But I got into trouble and they accused me of this.

*Had you ever been in any trouble before this?*
Yes. In Leesburg, Florida I got in trouble.

*What was that all about?*
Destroying Bell's telephone. And that was it. I tried to get the money out of the box and by doing that I destroyed the phone.

*Did you do any time for that?*
Yes they gave me three years.

*Three years for destroying a telephone?*
And that's the only time, . . . the only trouble I've been in. First time.

*What was it like those three years?*
Had to work on the roads and in the woods. The first one out there had to use these sling blades to cut grass with. Boss Young would walk up behind you and put his foot in your gut and kick you, hit you up side the head, cuss you and call you all kinds of names. It was rough. Your hands would be bleeding but you still had to work. If you didn't work they put you in a box, take off your clothes and put you in there for seven days. Your hands are all bloody, you could peel the skin off, but if you couldn't pick up the sling blade and cut grass with it, they put you in the box. Out of three years I didn't do but a year. But I didn't do it all on the road because I could cut hair too. So they put me inside to cut hair.

*Tell me about your arrest in South Carolina. What was that all about?*
The reason they arrested us was they said they had an all-points bulletin out on a blue and white car. My brother and me was driving a blue and white car and they stopped us and

arrested us. There were four of us in the car at the time but they just arrested my brother and me. I thought they were stopping us because I was smoking a joint. But they didn't even say nothing about that. I didn't know what to think then.

*Did they tell you why they were stopping you?*
They told my brother they had an all-points bulletin out on a blue and white car. That's what my brother told me when he got back in the car. And that's all I know about it.

They took us to the Aiken County jail. I went to sleep inside the place. I don't know how long I'd been asleep, it wasn't long. And that's when some guys came from Lexington County saying that we was charged with armed robbery-murder. They handcuffed us and brought us back to Lexington County. Slapped the handcuffs on us, took us in a car and brought us back to Lexington County, booked us, fingerprinted us, took pictures and locked us in a cell.

I didn't feel really bad 'cause I didn't do nothing. Most of the time I was sleeping a lot and I didn't have time to think anyway. I can't say I felt bad, I can't say I felt good. I didn't feel anything because I didn't have time to think.

*When did you get time to think? When did it hit you?*
When did it hit me? I guess that's when the lawyer came. That was about seven, eight days later. That's when they called our lawyer and that's when it hit me.

*During the trial did you think you would be convicted and sentenced to death?*
I knew if I was found guilty they were gonna give me the death penalty. That's what they were asking for. But I didn't have it in mind I was gonna get it. I thought it was gonna be thrown out because I didn't do nothing and the evidence they had was nothing. They didn't have any evidence.

*Do you think about the chance you'll be electrocuted?*
Yes, I think about that sometimes. But I try not to think about it. I think that, no, I'll never go to the electric chair. I put it in my mind and heart that I won't get electrocuted. Whatever come down I won't get electrocuted.

*You mean you'd take your own life first?*
No, never, never.

*So it's just that you're not going to think about being put in the electric chair.*

Right. The way I see it that's the only way you can deal with it is not to think about it. Put it in your mind that you'll be out of here one day. That's what I do and I get along pretty good by thinking that way.

My time in here has been pretty rough. But the less you think the better off you'll be. The less you think about going to the electric chair the better off you'll be. When John Spenkelink was executed that hit me pretty hard for about a day or two. Then I started thinking and stuff, trying to get this out of my mind.

*What's it been like going through all this with your brother?*

That's really got next to me because my brother is only 24 now. I had been in jail before for destroying that Bell telephone. And I felt that it was real bad on him because he knew nothing about prison. I didn't know if he was thinking like me or not about not letting it get next to him. Just put the best on the outside. Those putting the best on the outside and holding the worst on the inside can still have their body weakened, you know. But I still think that it was worse on him and that's making me feel kind of bad, too, by him being here. I'd feel a lot better if he wasn't in here.

*What's it been like for your mother? Does she come and see you?*

Yes. Twice a month. That's the only time she can come. Every two weeks. And she comes all the time. My mother felt bad at first but now she doesn't feel bad. She feels the same way I feel, that one day we'll be out of here.

*Was the victim's family in the courtroom when you were tried?*

Yes they were in there.

*Did they want you to get the death penalty?*

Oh yeah. They kept making faces at me. I just looked down. When we had a recess and I was going to the restroom, his wife, I guess that was his wife, she went in her purse and started after me hollering. Some of the people grabbed her and held her back. I just kept walking. Ever since I knowed myself I always try not to let anything worry me. When my common law wife said she was gonna leave me I let that get next to me. I cried. And then I started thinking about it and realized there was nothing I could do about it. If I could have done something about it I would have. So from then on I tried not to let anything worry me.

# David Washington

There is every likelihood that by the time you read these words David Washington will have been executed.

In September of 1976 David Washington killed three people in three different incidents. The police finally traced a check from one of the victims to Washington's house and arrested his brother, thinking him the murderer. Washington turned himself in, confessed to the murders, waived his rights to a jury trial and was convicted and sentenced before a judge when he pleaded guilty. He was sentenced to the electric chair and went to death row at the Florida State Prison in Starke in November of 1976. An appeal of his sentence has been to the U. S. Supreme Court and has been rejected. It appears that only a recommendation by the Clemency Board could keep David Washington from state-imposed death. That recommendation seems highly unlikely.

The law has little room for confession and repentance. A person convicted of a crime while proclaiming his innocence all the while is given the same treatment as a person convicted of a crime who confesses his guilt. Our legal system is not so fine-tuned that it can discriminate sincerity. David Washington went before a judge, confessed to three murders, was advised of his rights and was sentenced to die. The judge could have shown mercy in the sentencing but in this case did not.

David Washington didn't seem all that concerned with how the legal system considered his confession as we talked in a visiting room at Florida State Prison on a fall afternoon. Soft-spoken and calm he worked the index fingers of his big basketball hands into the shape of a steeple and talked repeatedly of how he hoped his confession was received by God. He said he didn't want to die. He said he couldn't understand why, if he was already restrained, he should be put to death. But he said he was prepared, he had taken his confession to the only authority he recognized as having the power to judge and pardon.

The sun, that afternoon, slid in and out of clouds and occasionally cut through the venetian blinds. Small swords of hard light struck David Washington as he spoke. He didn't notice them. He didn't stop to look at the activities in the outer office. He sat down and told me he was guilty of his crimes and he was on death row to pay for those crimes.

He paused twice. His brother and a friend had watched one of his victims for him and, though they did not participate in any murder, were each given three life sentences for their knowledge of the crimes. When speaking of how he had ruined their lives as well as the victims' he began to cry. I had heard from a guard that he cried often in his cell but I was not prepared. Everything about a men's prison, even the offices we were in, is hard-bitten, tough, and tightly-wound. The tears David Washington shed in that office and his attempt to shut them off quickly were painful to watch. I couldn't accept such extreme vulnerability in those surroundings. We sat in silence while he cried, wiped his eyes and continued.

The second time he paused was when he thought that what he was saying might hurt someone. He had told me time and time again that he did not want to die but if that was what the state of Florida required of him, so be it. I asked him if he thought that his attitude and eventual execution might not make it easier for the state of Florida to execute the other 130 men on death row with him. I asked the question as we were doing photographs. He stopped and stared. His expression didn't change at all. Slowly he looked at me. One of those little swords of light sliced across his cheek. "I hope the things I said don't hurt anybody," he said. "I hope you can see I want to do everything in my power against the death penalty and still be open and honest with you."

David Washington comes from a family of eight children. Most of his childhood was spent with his grandmother. His mother, according to him, went through three or four marriages. He speaks of his present stepfather as his father. At the age of seventeen he was sentenced to a juvenile center for breaking and entering. Part of the year and a half he did on that sentence was done in adult institutions and he spent some time in a hard labor camp. His second arrest was for the three murders that occurred in September 1976.

I suppose David Washington makes it easier for proponents of the death penalty to sleep. He is guilty and admits it. There is no chance we are executing an innocent person. He had no trial, so it appears there can be little dickering over the legal points raised in his case. He is prepared to accept his punishment. He is not going to make a scene as he is taken to his death. And he says, normally enough, that he does not want to die. Unlike the case of Gary Gilmore we will not be participating in a suicide by executing David Washington.

But making David Washington's acquaintance was an unsettling experience. The fundamental question raised by the death penalty, that of the state's right to execute its own, dominated our conversation whether we were speaking of it directly or not. The business of executing this man seems either feudal and bloodthirsty or futile and indifferent, the latter being the most odious.

I think often of that patch of light on David Washington's cheek. It reminds me of a blaze on a tree in the woods, a mark put there to show direction. I can read a blaze in the woods well enough and find

my way, but that patch of light was something different. His case is so open and shut and the state of Florida is so determined to execute those on its death row that I don't think I'll ever see him again. But his case is really *too* open and shut, his contrition too sincere, for there not to be serious and horrible questions about the damage his death will do to us all. And David Washington is but one in a growing forest of people on death row.

I GOT LAID OFF at the time my wife was in her ninth month, getting ready to have a baby. They laid me off and they started giving me an unemployment check. That ran out and I was on food stamps. But that don't cover rent and all that, you know living in Miami is really expensive.

I had all the opportunities to get a job. I took advantage of a lot of those opportunities. But after I got the job I would only work six or seven months. I was halfway doing right by my family but I was running the street. Running around with every woman I saw. Seemed like I always lived in a fantasy world. I always wanted to be somebody that I wasn't. I was always in the bright lights with the "let's get up and party" people. To be honest I couldn't leave the house and walk across the street 'less I run into somebody I know I had went with. I'd be scared to walk out of the house with my wife.

A lot of people find it hard to believe but I never in my life used any type of drugs or smoked cigarettes or drank beer or anything like that. I was pretty straight. I was just ignorant, you know.

And I was frustrated. My wife had just had that baby. You know how in-laws is. I wasn't good enough for their daughter as far as they were concerned. No way. And now that I look at it I wasn't no good, you know.

All these murders happened in that same year and they all happened in about a thirty day span. The first murder was the Pridgett murder. He was supposedly a minister. He was a black guy that lived in the neighborhood. He was a homosexual.

I was trying to think of a way to get some money, get the hell out of the house and get my own place. They gave us so many days to get out of the apartment we rented. They were going to set all the furniture outdoors. I didn't have Pampers to put on the baby's behind or nothing. I went to the wash house in my neighborhood one day and this preacher was there washing his clothes, Daniel Pridgett. I don't know whether you know anything about gay people or homosexuals. He was just standing around and I'm just sitting there, just watching the sights, just letting my mind wander. He walked up to me and sat down and struck up a conversation. Then he hit on me in that ol' funny way, you know. Started talking this homosexual talk. And he told me he was a minister, you know, and that just made me mad. He hit on me while I was trying to get some money.

So I made a date with him and I went to his house that night. I was supposed to straddle him and he was supposed to anal or something. . . . I don't know what kind of sex you call it. I was supposed to straddle him and he was supposed to eat me and I just stabbed him with a knife. I stabbed him about five times. The only thing was going through my mind I said, "Here I am out here trying to get some money to feed my family and here go a minister, supposed to be a minister in the church, running around doing stuff like this." I just got mad and just stabbed him. I don't know where my life went wrong, man.

The second one was the old lady. There were four ladies in the house. They used to buy a lot of hot merchandise from blacks out of the neighborhood. It was her and her husband and it was like a big old store hooked onto the house. And they'd buy all kinds of stolen TV's and things like that.

Well I went in there to hold them up that night. There was four of them sitting around in chairs. I told everybody just to be still until they'd give me the money. I had the gun in my hand. I was scared. I was shaking and waiting. I told them all to just lay on the floor. I was trying to tie them up and one got up and she was walking around behind me. I just panicked. I looked around and I was shooting up the place. And I left people messed up all kind of ways.

The last one was a University of Miami student. I took about $80 from him, out of his wallet. When I stabbed him I started crying. He was saying the Lord's prayer over and over again and I just stood and I was crying. My mind just went blank. It seemed like I was the onliest one on this planet. I was screaming for help and nobody would help. I was just lost in this world.

I didn't know what I was doing. I never hid out. They really didn't know who they was looking for. They got hold of my baby brother. I had gone to the bank and cashed a check, a $2500 check from the University of Miami student. They tracked the taxi driver to where I lived. They got my brother. They broke into the house and took my brother and I was ten to fifteen miles on the other side of town at the time they did that. But they thought they was looking for my brother, they didn't know anything about me. So Mama told me what had happened. I walked into the police station. I confessed to everything. I was guilty of all three of those murders. They convicted my brother, Nathaniel Taylor and a friend Johnny Mills just because they knew what I was doing. Wasn't nobody present when I killed anybody. On the University of Miami student they knew what was taking place. They was even in the house when I brought the boy there but after that, that was it. Now I feel like in a way everybody supposed to get what's coming to them. Maybe they were supposed to get some time. But three life sentences and 25 years?

If you're my brother I ain't gonna let you go to jail for something you ain't did. A lot of guys don't look at it like that but I'd give my life for any member of my family, a thousand times over. I had close to $2,000 on me at the time I found out them people had my brother locked up down there. I could have been half way across the world somewhere. Instead I tried to save my brother. They had me in one room spilling my guts, trying to save him. They had my brother in another room beating him all upside the head, kicking him, throwing him all over the floor and he's telling them what little that he did know.

My brother and Johnny Mills was just around me at the wrong time. I told them, "Just watch the guy for me." Doing something against their will you know. Man, I look back to then. You'd be surprised the people's lives I messed up.

*And the victims?*

Hey, man, that's the only thing. I lay up in bed sometimes and I just cry. I just cry and cry 'cause it's always on my conscience. I think about the people's lives I took. Sometimes I wake up in the middle of the night and I say, "Damn, I took three people's lives," and I just start crying. You got 125 or 130 men on death row and out of 125 you might find two or three that will come out and tell you that they're guilty of the crimes they're here for. The time's out for playing games now, you understand what I'm saying. I feel bad. I don't know what to say.

I wish it hadn't happened. I feel sorry for the things I did and I tell anybody if taking my life gonna satisfy somebody, well take it. I don't want to die, but then again I didn't have the right to take these peoples' lives, you understand what I'm saying? I ain't going to go out there and tell these people to take my life, but if they say, "David Washington, it's your time to die," I'm gonna say, "Just come on with it. I'm ready for it." I think my life was just one big mistake. I had all the best breaks in life, all the right opportunities. Seemed like everything I touched, I destroyed. Family, wife, friends, everything. I just destroyed.

I didn't have no jury trial or nothing. I went right before the judge and told him what I told the detectives. I was guilty of all the crimes. He asked if I understood my rights and this and that and I told him, "Yeah," and that was it. I came to death row around November '76.

I put myself here. I can deal with that. I don't want to die but I'm here for one reason, to pay for my crimes. I ask the Lord to forgive me for my sins. Some people say, "Well, it's a little late for that." The way I look at it it's never too late. I'm human. I really don't worry about that outside world. I really don't worry about what happens to me now. As long as I get my life right and try and make the best of it now is all that matters.

I see my mistakes. I see where I went wrong. I've basically been a liar, a cheat and a thief all my life. Here I am now facing death. A lot of people don't believe in God but I do believe in God. If I'm going to come to you and tell you a lie and go to Him and get on my knees and be honest with Him, what do you call that? I'm lying on one end but I'm being truthful on the other. If I'm going to be right with God I might as well be right with you. Can you understand what I'm saying? So either I'm going to reject God and tell you all these lies or I'm gonna be right with God and right with you too.

*Let's talk about how you grew up. Where were you born?*

I was born in Trenton, New Jersey December 13, 1949. I think we moved from Trenton when I was 10 years old. I've been in Miami off and on all my life.

*And did you grow up with your parents?*

Basically it was back and forth from my mother to my grandmother. I enjoyed living with my mother so much that I just decided to stay with her but my grandmother raised me. She was in Miami.

*And your father?*

It's kind of hard to say. I never really got a chance to know my father. I come from a large family, five brothers and two sisters. My mother's been married three or four different times. My stepfather was a pretty nice guy. He lived with us. I'm the oldest of seven kids.

With seven kids running around the house my mother couldn't just put all her attention on me. And she was working too. But I'm saying the time she did have, she gave it to me the best she could as far as trying to keep me in school, clothes and stuff like that.

As far as growing up, I basically had all the opportunities any other kid had. I didn't come from a real strict family. Maybe that had something to do about where I went wrong.

*How did your schooling go?*

I didn't have any trouble in school but I never got farther than the tenth grade. Right around graduation time in the tenth grade I got locked up and I received a five year sentence for breaking and entering, and that ended my school. I did about 18 months at the Appalachia Correctional Institute.

*Was that your first arrest?*

That was the first and this is the second time. I did my eighteen months and I was on parole. I was nineteen. I got me a nice job and I went to work. I don't think I was on the street a hot year before I was married.

I was young. I was in there so fast and it seemed like I was on the street so fast I didn't know what happened to me.

I ain't never been happy. Things I wanted to do, seem like I never got a chance to do 'em. I was only happy when I was participating in sports. Football, basketball, track. I always wanted to be like a superstar. Always wanted to be like the Dr. J's and the Earl the Pearl's. I would look around and see the things and people that I envied and admired. Even though I wasn't those people I would go to the store and I would buy these jerseys and shirts and the emblems and stuff like that and I would wear them. I would sit up and fantasize about people like Earl the Pearl, Dr. J, "Pistol" Pete Maravich. I would just fantasize being people like that. When I was married, I just got married to be married, really. Just because she was a nice girl. It seemed like I always wanted to be something I wasn't. I tried to enlist for the service but I flunked the test. I always wanted to be everything that I wasn't.

With a tenth grade education I had all the best jobs you can think of. I used to work for the city of Miami at the incinerator. I was making good money. It was union. I used to work at Jordan Marsh, Sears and Roebuck, Winn Dixie, Food Fair. You can check all this on my record.

*Is there a reason why you had a lot of different jobs?*

I was a young man looking for something in life and really didn't know what I was looking for. I'd get tired of this job and I'd just quit and go on to the next job. There's really no excuse. . . .

*You said you liked to party. Were you running with a wild crowd?*

That's something I never did was run with a crowd or group. I participated in a lot of different sports and stuff like that. I never really started committing any crimes till September '76. And it was my fault then.

*You don't blame anyone or anything but yourself?*

I guess I would have to say I blame myself. And I would have to put a little bit of responsibility to some of my family, and society.

*Has your mother ever said anything to you about her responsibility?*

No. Never. I love my Mama. I respect her now. I was ignorant in a lot of areas and so was she. She didn't have time. If she spent all her time with us trying to show us where we were going right or wrong we would never have had food on the table and a place to stay.

*Are you blaming the economy to some extent for . . .?*

Not in my case. In some sense black mothers and fathers are stronger than white mothers and fathers 'cause they grew up with going hungry and they grew up with going home and struggling and surviving. You understand what I'm saying? I could go out there right now and say, "Mama, I'm going to try to make me some money because I'm tired of going hungry, I'm tired of being broke." She wouldn't want me to go and she'd try to stop me but if I'm going anyway she's gonna say, "Baby, be careful." If I came in the house with $300, $400, $500 the majority of upper class white parents would turn this money in. But I am gonna split this money with my Mama. And she's gonna take it and do the things that need to be done with it. My Mama didn't want me out there committing no crimes. She wanted me to do the things that was right. She always wanted me to be like my younger brother. He serves in the Air Force. That's her pride and joy. But I just went down the long road at night and it seemed like I got so far gone I couldn't turn around.

I wouldn't obey my Mama. I didn't give her the respect she deserved. If I ain't gonna respect her ain't nothing she can tell me but, "Be careful," you understand what I'm saying? But my Mama, my father, they tried to give me love and understanding the best they knew how. A lot of the things they told me went in one ear and right out the other ear. They didn't have the time to spend with me like a lot of parents have to spend with their child. The time they did have they tried to give to me but I rejected it. I felt like I knew everything. I didn't want to hear. I'm gonna live my own life. I guess I felt like I knew everything but really I didn't know nothing.

*Have your parents stuck with you?*

When everybody else lets you down your Mama and Daddy gonna be right there. They've been by my side from the very beginning. I tell my Mama I made my bed hard so I'm gonna lay on it by myself. But my Grandmama is old and my Mama tells me I'm going to kill her if I don't let her come see me. She basically raised me and I'm closer to her than anyone else. If I don't let her come and see me she's gonna worry anyway. So I try to ease the burden on her. I let her come up and see me every now and then.

*Are the visits hard for you?*

Visits aren't hard for me. But to me a visit ain't nothing but a pacifier. Some guys back there live for one day, just like a baby sucking on a bottle. They live for a visit, trimming their nails, brushing their hair. They live and they talk about just one day. I understand what they're facing. All they talk about is women, women, getting in this visiting parlor, what it's gonna be like when they get out there. And when the visit don't show up it's just like a baby crying on a bottle. They all done got frustrated. They're mad, want to know what went wrong. I made this bed hard for me to lay on. I am gonna lay on it by myself. I don't need this pacifier. I done caused my parents pain and suffering all my life and I'm tired of leaning on them. So it's time for me to give them a break now and stand on my own two feet. This is a load I want to carry by myself. I've made it, so I want to carry it. I try to make them understand but then again I've come to realize a lot of things since I've been here. I try to give my parents a little more respect now than I did then. I don't reject them as far as visits. I try to keep it down a little bit. I let them come up to see me maybe once a month, once every other month.

*What about the families of the victims?*

If there was anything, short of selling my soul to the devil, I could do to bring them back to their families or stop the suffering or pay back what I did, I would be willing to do it. But I know there ain't no way I can do that. I'm always thinking about these people I killed, every day, every day. That's why it just don't bother me if these people take my life.

I'm not going to come out here and say, "All right take my life,

I want to die, I'm sick of living in this cell. If I got to live like this take my life." You understand what I'm saying? But then again I ain't gonna come out here and play no games with you. I'm here because of my crimes. I don't want to die. I don't think it's right what you people are doing in the state of Florida. But I really don't have no say-so. They don't want to hear nothing I got to say.

*It sounds like you're saying that if you go to the electric chair, that will pay for your crimes.*

I don't think it will pay for it. But if these people think it's gonna pay for it, if they are gonna get some kind of self-satisfaction out of it, take my life. I don't have any reason to fight it and I won't fight it because I'm guilty for my crimes. If the state of Florida says that's the way you got to pay for your crimes, well, I'm ready. I'm willing to give my life that way for it. As far as this gonna do any good, I really don't think it's gonna do any good 'cause crime was here from the beginning. It's gonna be here till the end.

*Do you think there is some way you could say that the people back there on death row don't deserve to live because they are animals?*

No. I think society is the animal. We are already in cages, man. They already took us away from society. What else can we do to them? They're still not satisfied. They just want to see us dead. They felt like they done run out of activities to do so they just kill some people on death row.

I stop and think, "We're animals now," but look at those people out there. Bloodthirsty, trying to take our lives. We're already locked up but they still want to see us dead. I can't see that being nothing else but animal behavior. We are the ones who supposed to be the animals. I hear a lot of them say they are Christians but yet they still want to see us dead.

I really don't believe a Christian can say he's a Christian and take another human life or stand by, if there's any power, to watch somebody take another human being's life. That's some kind of Christian. That's got to be Satan. That's got to be the devil. That's not a Christian as far as I'm concerned.

*Where are you in the appeals procedure now?*

My case went through the courts, Florida Supreme, United States Supreme Court, as far as I know twice. It was in and out just like that. I was talking to a lawyer about it a couple of months ago and she told me that I'd probably go before the

Clemency Board somewhere within the next year. To be honest with you I don't think I'll see December 1980.

*What does death look like to you from where you are now?*
What does it look like to me? It looks like a joke to me. It might sound to you like I say some stupid things but . . .

*You're not afraid to die?*
No. I used to be. But I'm not afraid to die any more.

*When did that change?*
After I gave my life to Christ. See, most of the guys I know up there they do a lot of praying. But they're not praying for their souls. They're praying for one thing: "Oh Lord, if you just spare me and get me life in prison and commute my sentence . . ." Do you understand what I'm saying? Basically they got their mind on that world out there. One more crack at that world. But I'm still thinking I have to face the Lord. Now death's staring me in the face. I'm not asking these people to take my life. But I ain't gonna sit out here and tell you no bunch of lies. I'm just gonna tell you the truth. I ain't gonna play no games with you. I'm guilty.

*I've noticed that you can't remember the name of the woman you killed and have trouble remembering which murder came first.*
I try to block out my past but it's constantly on my mind. I took people's lives in this world that didn't deserve to die. I try to block all of this stuff out. I try to block it out but it keeps coming back to me. The transcripts of my case are laying there on the desk and I just happen to look around and know what they are and there it is. They're right there in those papers. I watch a movie on TV and see a lady hard at work and I think about this lady. She was a hard worker, she was just trying to make a living.
Sometimes I wake up all fresh, like I'm laying out in a bunch of roses. And I look up and the first thing pops into my mind is, "Damn, I took three people's lives." I look at the bars and realize where I am. Sometimes when you wake up you don't realize where you're at. I look at the bars and the first thing that comes to my mind is that I took three people's lives, I killed some people. And I start crying.

*Do you think about the electric chair often?*
A man asked me the other day (it was a stupid question as far as I'm concerned) if I had a chance of taking a lethal injection or the electric chair, which one would I choose. I said, "You killed

my brother John Spenkelink, you didn't give him no chance, I'm gonna die just like he died. Death is death regardless of which way you die. Don't give me no break. You didn't give him a break."

*You knew John Spenkelink well?*
We were close friends. He was like a leader. Around here these officers believe when you got a leader like him you kill the head and the body's gonna die. So they tried to keep him isolated. When you had a problem or you couldn't reason with something, you could always go to him. He was calm. He was quiet. If we wanted to get some changes done around here and get them done right, we just got together with him and he'd make sure it's right.

In some ways I feel like he wasn't prepared to die because he had more faith in those lawyers than he had in God. If he'd had the faith in God that he had in those lawyers he probably would have stood a better chance of not dying in that chair. I don't know whether you can understand what I'm saying. His lawyers might not understand. He felt like in a way that these lawyers would save him at the last minute.

I put all my faith in God. I don't care nothing about the lawyers. I appreciate and respect everything they are trying to do for me. And I ain't going to tell them to stop working on my case or nothing like that. But if they do everything they can do for me and that's it, well I'm ready for it.

*What about the people you know here on death row? Are they ready for it?*
Some of the guys say they'd live their life the same way, they'd just be a little slicker and a little wiser. But a lot of the guys have seen their whole life pass before them and they know. I believe they are sincere when they say if they had one more chance in life there is no way they would live it the way they had lived it. It would be a totally different thing. You get to know a lot of guys. You come to love a lot and then a lot you want to hate. Death row is the same every day. You wake up with death on your mind and you go to sleep with death on your mind. You watch TV twenty-four hours a day. All they eat, sleep and talk is the death sentence. Some guys haven't prepared themselves for what's coming.

*How did you prepare yourself?*
I got one thing. I believe in God. I believe he is the only person who can and will forgive me for all these sins and crimes I've

committed. I go to Him in prayer, just like I come to you and I tell you everything I did. I go to him with an open heart, with all honesty and I tell him everything. I worry about my soul. I don't want to lose my soul. I don't care about my life. If they want to take it, let them take it. I feel like I owe society something. I don't want to die but then again I ain't got no reason to say don't take my life. It ain't gonna solve nothing, but if it's gonna give them some kind of justice, well, take my life. I'm more scared of losing my soul than I am my life. I do bad things every day but that's human nature. I curse. I get on the door and scream and holler and crack jokes with the guys. I'm basically trying to make peace with the Lord. I'm prepared in that way. I do believe my time's coming. I'm not gonna get a stay of execution, I really honestly believe that. I laid everything right out on the table. At the time when I first got here I was scared. I was really scared. But in one sense I wasn't. I knew what things I did wrong and I feel like I owe society something. But there's got to be a better way than what they're doing.

# Watt Espy: The Historical Perspective

Watt Espy is an independent researcher in Tuscaloosa, Alabama who has made it his life's work to chronicle all the legal executions that have ever taken place in the United States. An historian with a passion for accuracy and detail, Watt goes about his task with the thoroughness of a scientist and the zeal of a missionary. When I visited him in his small office he told me right away how he had come to his rather unusual occupation.

> "I have always been a stickler for detail and facts and things being correct. I got so damned tired of reading that somebody was executed in 1870 when I knew it happened in 1850 that I said, 'Well, my God, surely there's a listing somewhere that shows all of them.' I found out there wasn't and I was horrified. Now here we are, we've taken these lives, they're human lives, and yet we've thought so little of them that we've never really made a listing, a chronicle of them, or found out how many we've taken. I know it's going to be impossible to confirm them all, I don't have any illusions about that, but I'm going to attempt to confirm just as many as I can."

When, in the summer of 1979, the Alabama Senate was considering a bill to abolish capital punishment, Watt Espy testified before the judicial committee. The amount of time he was told he would have to deliver his remarks was cut drastically the day he appeared and he was forced to abbreviate his statement. The full text of that testimony is worth reading:

> I appreciate having the opportunity of testifying before you during your deliberations on this human piece of legislation which seeks to abolish capital punishment in our state—something which has been done in practically every civilized country, with the notable exceptions of certain states in the United States and the Government of the Republic of South Africa.
>
> By way of introduction I would like to tell you something of my research for the past seven years which, I believe, qualifies me to discuss the subject now being considered by your distinguished committee. My work entails research into the history of capital punishment in our country and hopefully will culminate in the publication of a series of volumes which will contain listings of all legal executions to have taken place in the United States,

including as many documented facts as possible on those executed and their crimes.

My work is entirely objective and does not seek to present a brief for or against capital punishment. Indeed, when I started it some seven years ago, I had personally formed no fixed opinions on the subject. However, as my research progressed and certain facts, inequities and injustices became obvious to me I became convinced that I am unalterably opposed to it. In addition to the moral repugnance that all civilized men have towards the taking of human life, even under the most aggravating of circumstances, the death penalty has always been used in a discriminating and unfair manner and has never served its avowed purpose of being a deterrent to other acts of violence.

Indeed, I am convinced, to some extent at least, that the exact contrary is true. It actually increases violence in that it is a demonstration, condoned by the executing governmental authority, of a depressing lack of appreciation for the intrinsic value of all human life and therefore has a naturally demoralizing effect on the population in general.

At this time I have confirmed a total of 11,334 legal executions that have taken place in the geographical area now comprising the United States of America since the first, which was that of Daniel Frank who was hanged in the Colony of Virginia on March 1, 1622, for stealing a calf and other chattels belonging to Sir George Yeardley. This work is far from complete as I would estimate that there have been between 18,000 and 20,000 human beings to have paid the supreme penalty during the ensuing 357 years. I would also like to add that such important information as races, ages, educations, occupations, etc. have not yet been obtained on all of the 11,334 confirmed executions. But this information has been obtained on a sufficient number for certain observations and conclusions to be formed on a tentative basis. Let me begin those observations and conclusions by addressing the issue of the death penalty as a deterrence.

The argument we most often hear in favor of capital punishment is that it is a deterrent to crime. In my opinion the only person who it really deters is the man who is executed. Certainly he will never sin again. There are simply too many cases of persons who knew the awful fate prescribed by the law in capital cases but who, nonetheless, committed crimes that resulted in their being put to death themselves.

J. Samuel McCue was a prominent attorney in Charlottesville, Virginia who, in addition to serving as the Mayor of Thomas Jefferson's hometown, had also served as an attorney in many capital cases, both as a prosecutor and as defense counsel. He well knew the penalty for murder and yet, on February 10, 1905, he was hanged in Charlottesville for the murder of his wife.

During his tenure as Sheriff of Allegheny County, Maryland, George Swearingen had hanged several convicted felons. He certainly knew the terrors of the gallows where, in most instances, persons were not spared the merciful death of having their necks broken but instead slowly strangled to death—in some instances for as long as thirty minutes, retaining consciousness until almost the very end. In spite of this knowledge of the consequences of murder, George Swearingen was, himself, hanged at Cumberland on October 2, 1829 for having murdered his wife.

Charles Justice, an inmate electrician at the Ohio State Prison around the turn of the century installed the electric chair at that institution. Released on parole, he killed a policeman, was tried, convicted and on October 27, 1911 he expiated his crime in the very chair he had constructed and wired.

On October 8, 1875, a black man named George Speer was legally hanged at Fayetteville, Georgia for the rape of a white girl. Among witnesses of this execution was Speer's natural brother, Clarke Edmundson (the difference in names results from the fact that, prior to emancipation, they belonged to different owners). Four days after Speer's execution, Edmundson raped a white woman, was captured and lodged in the Fayetteville Jail from whence he was taken by a mob on the night of October 17 and hanged from the same gallows from which his brother had been executed nine days earlier.

I shall burden you with but one other example of one who knew the awful penalty for murder but was not deterred, though there are hundreds of others. On August 24, 1827, a man named Jesse Strang was publicly hanged at Albany, New York. Among the witnesses was Levi Kelley, a prosperous farmer from Cooperstown. The execution made such a strong impression on Mr. Kelley that, after returning home, he remarked to a number of his neighbors that he did not believe that anyone who ever witnessed an execution could commit a murder through fear of being hanged himself. Ten days later this same Kelley shot and killed one of his tenants. This man on whom the execution of August 24 had made such a profound impression was then tried and condemned to die. On December 28, 1827, just four months after he had traveled to Albany to witness Strang's execution he was hanged himself. A tragic aftermath of the Kelley execution was the fact that, during the proceedings, one of the platforms erected so that witnesses could have a good view, collapsed and two persons were killed. Additionally, a neighbor and friend named Cooke became so depressed following the execution that one week later he committed suicide by hanging himself

Thank God we have gotten away from public executions, but if they are really intended to be deterrents to crime then it seems as though we should want to make them as public as possible. Public executions, with their grim, carnival horror, continued right on up until this century in some jurisdictions. The last two that I have recorded were those of Rainey Bethea, a black man, in Kentucky and Roscoe "Red" Jackson, a white man, at Galena, Missouri.

Bethea was convicted of the rape-murder of an aged white woman and on August 14, 1936, he paid with his life in a public spectacle at Owensboro, Kentucky. Thousands upon thousands of persons arrived from several states and their drunken decorum was so disgusting that the condemnation of the civilized world was brought down on the Commonwealth of Kentucky. It rapidly changed its law to read that future hangings should take place in private.

Missouri allowed public hangings up until 1937 when it passed a bill providing for the asphyxiation of those condemned to die at the State Prison. Roscoe Jackson, a 36-year-old drifter who claimed to be a great-nephew of General Stonewall Jackson, and who had murdered a friendly motorist who had given him a ride, had been sentenced under the old law and he thus goes down as the last man publicly hanged in a legal manner in the United States.

There were tragic aftermaths to virtually every public execution. On May 9, 1879, two black men, Tom Jones and Henry McLeod, were hanged at Appling, Columbia County, Georgia. Some white citizens of McDuffie County who had traveled to Appling to join the festivities got into a brawl immediately after the execution and twenty-five shots were fired. One man was fatally wounded and three others injured less seriously.

In June, 1889, a man named Alex Henderson was hanged at Bainbridge, Georgia. Henry Lindsey took his two young sons, one ten and the other thirteen, to witness the execution, no doubt believing that it would have some salutary effect. The youngest son, highly impressionable and religiously inclined, afterwards improvised a crude gallows in the cow pen by placing a plank at an angle to represent the scaffold and suspending a plowline from a scantling to serve as a noose. For several days he spent much of his time on this makeshift scaffold, repeating the religious services held at Henderson's execution, singing the hymns, and playing a game which he called "Henderson's hanging." On July 20, 1889 he did not return home for supper and when his mother went to the cow pen searching for him, she found his lifeless body hanging from the plowline.

While it is quite clear to me that the death penalty does not deter violent crime and can not be proven to do so and may in many cases foster violent behavior, there are other aspects of capital punishment which, to my way of thinking, make it an unacceptable form of punishment. Perhaps the most obvious aspect is that the death penalty is bound to be applied to innocent people no matter what our safeguards against such mistakes are.

I concede that most of the people who have been executed in this country have been guilty of the crimes for which they were convicted. However, there have been plenty of innocent people, subsequently proven innocent beyond a shadow of a doubt, to have been deprived of their lives by due process of law. In addition to those proven innocent after their execution there are others, I am sure, who were innocent but have never been proven to be so because law enforcement officials and prosecutors will not investigate a case once an execution has been held. The case is closed for them and it is probably too much to expect them to go out and try to prove that they have executed an innocent person no matter what the evidence.

To my way of thinking nothing can be more horrible or repugnant than that the state, with all its power for good or evil, should deprive one of its citizens of life for a crime committed by another. The examples are many. The father of U.S. Supreme Court Justice Lucius Quintius Cincinnatus Lamar, himself a brilliant Milledgeville, Georgia, jurist, once sentenced a Methodist minister to hang for the rape-murder of his sister-in-law. The judgement of the court was duly carried out and several years later Judge Lamar was in his office when he was informed that a message had just arrived from Mississippi that a man, hanged there for another crime, had confessed from the gallows to the crime for which the minister had been executed. So hurt was the judge that he locked his office, walked to his home, kissed the members of his family, including the future Supreme Court Justice who was then but a small child, goodbye, and shot himself through the head.

January 7, 1898, was hanging day in Greenfield, Massachusetts, for on that day Jack O'Neill became one of the last persons to be hanged in the Bay State which was soon to provide for the electrocution of its condemned. O'Neill was an Irishman, one of the immigrants hated in that state at that particular time, the same Irish strain that was later to give our country President John F. Kennedy. O'Neill, who maintained that he was innocent and was a victim of bigotry, had been convicted of the rape murder of Hattie Evelyn McCloud at Buckland on January 8, 1897. His last words were: "I shall meet death like a man and I hope those who see me hanged will live to see the day when it is proved that I am innocent—and it will some day." These prophetic words came true shortly afterwards when a soldier from Shelburne Falls, a member of the Sixth Massachusetts Militia, dying of wounds received in Cuba during the Spanish American War, confessed that he and not O'Neill had murdered Miss McCloud, furnishing details and information that only the actual killer could have known.

In Dutchess County, New York, in 1806, there was a drunken brawl at the home of Jesse Wood, a farmer, in which the participants were Wood and his two sons, Joseph and Hezekiah. A shotgun was fired and Joseph Wood fell dead. Hezekiah swore that his father had fired the gun and Jesse was duly arrested and convicted on Hezekiah's testimony. The old man claimed that he was too drunk to remember what had happened and he went to his death saying that while he might have killed Joseph, he did not recall it. Ten years later, as he lay dying, Hezekiah Wood confessed that he had fired the shot that killed his brother and admitted that he had perjured himself against his father to save his own life.

Of all the countries on the face of the earth, I feel that we have more safeguards to prevent the conviction of the innocent than probably any other, but this is not enough as the innocent are, on occasion, convicted. I cannot imagine any human being, who is not a perfect monster himself, viewing with unconcern the prospect of an innocent man being executed, but that possibility always exists where the death penalty is available.

Along with the execution of innocent people we must consider the execution of the insane. During the nightmare regime of Adolph Hitler in Germany the Jews were not the only persons to be liquidated. The insane and those who suffered from various mental and physical disorders were also shot, hanged, gassed and used for medical experiments. The civilized world recoiled in horror at this excessive use of death as an instrument of state policy. The argument will be advanced by those who advocate capital punishment that this has not and cannot happen in this country where statutes forbid the execution of those who are not mentally responsible for their acts of violence.

Yet insane persons have been executed in the United States. Where the man whose life is in jeopardy is penniless and friendless with no funds with which to employ adequate alienists to examine him and to testify for him, the only psychiatrists available have generally been those from state hospitals who, in all too many instances, have given only perfunctory examinations, frequently for as short periods as 15 minutes in the cell of the accused and who, in practically every instance have served as an extension of the prosecuting arm of the state, certifying a man to be rational and sane enough to be executed.

One of the most celebrated cases in American history of an obviously insane person being executed is the case of Albert Fish who was electrocuted by the state of New York on January 16, 1936. Fish, a 65-year-old house painter, was a member of a distinguished family which had furnished a Secretary of State of the United States, a United States Senator and several members of Congress. A religious fanatic, he was in and out of mental institutions for all of his adult life but nonetheless managed to father and raise a large family of children. At the time of his arrest for the murder of an 11-year-old girl, Grace Budd, he admitted to having eaten her flesh for a period of several days after he had killed her. He then calmly related that over the course of 20 years he had murdered and cannibalistically feasted off the bodies of numerous children of both sexes. This grandfatherly appearing old man was x-rayed and found to have no less than thirty needles of various sizes, including a large sailing needle, totally imbedded in his body in the regions of his abdomen and scrotum. Many of these needles had been inserted for so long a time that they had calcified. Thoroughly examined by the eminent alienist, Dr. Frederic Wertham, he was declared totally insane. In fact, Dr. Wertham said that there was no known perversion that Fish had not practiced at one time or another. Wertham presented a long list of these perversions which, in addition to the most extreme forms of sadism and masochism, included the fact that he had, over a long period of time, supplemented his diet with human feces. The state presented alienists from the state hospitals which had held Fish on numerous occasions, including twice after he had killed and eaten Grace Budd and they all said that they had released him after short periods of confinement because, while he was peculiar and eccentric, he was not insane. They testified that he was perfectly sane at the time of his crime and perfectly sane then. His conviction was affirmed on appeal and then a strong plea for executive clemency was made to Governor Herbert H. Lehman. Lehman, an avowed liberal who did much to further progressive causes in this country during a long and useful life, listened to the evidence. He then made a startling statement in which he expressed the opinion that Fish was insane but said that so horrible was his crime that he saw no alternative to allowing the law to take its course. This pathetic, sick old man went to the electric chair with an air of exhilaration, actually helping to strap himself to the instrument of death and explaining that he looked forward to the charge of electricity that would end his life as being the most powerful sexual stimulation that he had ever received.

I would also like to cite to you the case of Elmer N. Arrant who was the local manager for one of the State's major utility companies in Fort Deposit, Alabama. Arrant had a long record of mental instability and had, at one time, been a patient in a private sanitorium. Subject to delusions, he became convinced that one of his neighbors, John E. Norman, was having an affair with Mrs. Arrant. On the evening of June 20, 1935, he telephoned Norman and asked that he and Mrs. Norman step over to his house. When the Normans entered his yard, he shot and killed both of them from a place of concealment behind a tree. His defense was one of insanity but he was nonetheless convicted and the sentence of death pronounced. After the conviction had been affirmed, a strong effort was made to have the sentence commuted on the grounds of mental incompetancy, but Governor Bibb Graves declined to do so. The Governor conceded that Arrant was insane, but he said that Arrant had been in that condition for years and yet had been accepted as a leader of his community. On June 19, 1936, while murmuring a prayer, Elmer N. Arrant was electrocuted at Kilby Prison.

As long as the death penalty remains on the statutes there is always the possibility that people who are not responsible will be put to death by the State, which had an obligation to take care of them and to protect them from themselves and others. In so many cases the execution of the insane is the expedient and popular thing to do but it is never the right thing to do. If the state can kill an Albert Fish, the state can close down its mental hospital and set up a crematorium on the grounds, or a gas chamber, as Hitler did. I would like to add that I have only used these two illustrations for the sake of brevity. There are hundreds of other cases of persons who were insane and yet have been executed.

As Americans we are all indignant and condemnatory of the death penalty being used as a political tool in other countries. We consider it an abhorrent and barbaric practice. We say that it can never happen here but it has in the past and, as long as it remains an accepted form of punishment, it can happen again.

In the very early days of the Colonies the Puritans in Massachusetts passed a law, on October 19, 1658, which provided that every person of the "cursed sect of the Quakers" found within the colony "should be immediately imprisoned without fail and being convicted to be of the sect of Quakers, should immediately be banished on pain of death." We know that at least four persons were hanged in the Massachusetts Bay Colony because of the fact that they were Quakers.

On May 4, 1884, a labor rally was held in Chicago's Haymarket Square which was addressed by a number of labor organizers, some of whom were avowed anarchists. The meeting was heavily patrolled by policemen and this was highly and rightly resented by the workers who had gathered peacefully. Towards the conclusion of the rally a bomb was exploded and one policeman was instantly killed while six others subsequently died of their wounds. Albert Parsons and other leaders were arrested and four of them, Parsons, August Spies, George Engel and Adolph Fischer, were hanged on November 11, 1887, after having been tried and convicted. Other leaders of the workers were sentenced to varying prison terms though it was never proven that any of those convicted had any prior knowledge of the bomb.

There are many other examples of the death penalty having been used in our country as a means of political control. The case of Johnny Harris here in Alabama is presently being discussed the world over as one having political overtones. Personally I have not studied this case or the facts surrounding it to any extent, my work being primarily one of studying cases where the death penalty has actually been exacted, and I do not feel qualified to express any sentiments on it. However, rather than see the good name of Alabama criticized in such a fashion I would hope that this body or some similar legislative group would make an impartial study of the circumstances surrounding the entire affair.

Certainly wherever the death penalty is condoned and is recognized as a legitimate form of punishment, the potential is present for its misuse as a political weapon when placed in the wrong hands. This, of course, includes many over-zealous prosecutors and other politicians who have used the death penalty as a means of seeking higher political office. These men, generally speaking, are not necessarily bloodthirsty but they are inordinately ambitious. In many instances they have succeeded temporarily, but their constituents have usually seen through their lust for office and their successes have been short lived.

Governors Whitman of New York (the Becker case) and Dorsey of Georgia (the Leo Frank case) have met with such fate. Others have failed to obtain their highest ambitions because of their vigorous espousals of the death penalty, even in states where capital punishment is an accepted fact. There can be but little doubt that his hardened attitude was partially responsible for the defeat of Attorney General Shevin in the Florida Gubernatorial primaries last year by the more moderate Bob Graham who, nevertheless, now has the dubious distinction of having consented to the first non-consential execution in this country since 1967.

There are those who argue for the death penalty on the grounds that mercy should not be shown to one who has shown no mercy. These advocates of using the law as a means of vengeance instead of punishment are saying, in essence, that the law and government which should be the most exalted expression of man's noblest and most merciful thoughts and ideals, actually should reflect man's basest instinct—the desire and will to kill. Punishment for crime must be exacted, certainly and surely—about that there can be no doubt—but is the death penalty a fit and rational punishment? I say no, it is not. It does not restore life to the victim, nor does it restore the husband to the widow nor the parent to the orphan. The ends of justice are far better served, the sacredness of life affirmed instead of denied by the state and the possibility of some form of restitution remains with the abolition of capital punishment and the substitution of greater safeguards in the pardoning and parole process.

Perhaps the most disturbing aspect of the death penalty is that it is discriminately applied. There has always been discrimination in the application of capital punishment and as long as death penalty laws remain on the statutes there always will be. With but a few exceptions, members of minorities, the poor, the friendless, the uneducated and, if you will pardon the expression, "the different" are the ones who pay with their lives for their crimes.

The black man who killed the white man has always been more likely to pay with his life than the white man who has killed the black man. This has been universally true in every state in this Union, not just the South. In my research, that is in over 11,000 cases, I can recall only two where white men were hanged for murders of black men. One occurred in the state of Georgia in the 1870's and the other in the state of Mississippi in the 1890's. Both of these white men were more or less outcasts, thoroughly despised by their white neighbors, one because he was a gambler and whiskey dealer, the other because he was considered a rouge in general, and both because they chose blacks for their closest friends.

My work has shown me fairly conclusively that economics enter into the application of the death penalty. Only rarely has a man been executed for the murder of someone belonging to a lower social or economic order. However where one has killed his social or economic superior, he has practically been assured of atoning for his transgression with his life. The poor, of course, suffer most in this situation, having to rely on court-appointed attorneys for their defense. Once they are convicted they have not the means to afford a prolonged fight for life. Generally the poor do not have powerful and influential friends to seek executive clemency for them. They are simply forgotten except for their family and loved ones, whose suffering is, of course, intense. I have found cases where relatives and loved ones have died of grief or have committed suicide.

Let me conclude my comments on the discriminatory nature of the death penalty by mentioning a contemporary case. We are all familiar with the case of Dan White, the former San Francisco policeman and city councilman, an accepted member of the "establishment" who entered the San Francisco city hall through a back window with a loaded revolver and shot Mayor George Mosconi and Councilman Harvey Milk to death. White promptly surrendered himself to the police at the station where he had previously been employed, wept and pleaded insanity, claiming that he had not meant to kill but offering no reason for sneaking into the offices armed. He was convicted of manslaughter and received a seven year sentence after entering a plea of insanity. The same week that he was convicted, in the same state, California, another killer—a drifter who had killed several people and drank their blood—who also pleaded insanity but was convicted of first-degree murder and sentenced to be executed in the gas chamber. To my way of thinking White's crime was one of premeditated murder if there ever has been one. Also to my way of thinking one who drinks human blood, believing himself to be some sort of vampire or Dracula, is obviously insane and not a fit candidate for the gas chamber. No other illustration could more dramatically show the injustice of the death penalty even today when we have the most stringent safeguards possible ordered by the Federal courts and written into law by the various legislatures. Different juries try different cases and, being different, they weigh the evidence with different sets of scales. Different judges decide on degrees of mitigation and they "march to the tune of different drummers." I would like to echo a statement attributed to the Marquis de Lafayette who is reported to have said, "I shall ask for the abolition of the penalty of death until I have the infallibility of human judgement demonstrated to me."

To summarize, I would urge you to report from your committee this bill to abolish capital punishment in our state. I would do so because the death penalty, a throwback to a less enlightened era, serves no useful purpose. It is not a deterrent to crime nor does it restore life to the victim. It is demoralizing to the population in general in that it shows a lack of regard for the sanctity of human life by the State itself. Finally the possibility of error exists and I am certain that each of you will agree with me that nothing can be more terrible or more reprehensible than for the state to unjustly take the life of one of its own citizens. Someday the death penalty will be eradicated in the United States and we will look back on it as a part of our Dark Ages, just as we now look back on the hanging of witches at Salem as an abomination we can no longer tolerate. If mankind is to survive on this planet we must learn to live together and be civilized. The death penalty is not civilized. Let its demise begin with us.

# Appendix A    Organizations

Listed below are organizations that I found to be useful sources of information on the death penalty. All of them are abolitionist groups but most of them catalogue articles and books both for and against capital punishment. To my knowledge there is no single-issue group that exists to promote capital punishment, but there are a number of multi-purpose civic and political groups that are proponents of the death penalty.

I have listed here only the major interdenominational groups that oppose the death penalty. With the exception of the Mormons every major religious body that I am aware of is on record in opposition to the sentence of death. That includes Protestant, Catholic and Jewish groupings.

National Coalition Against the Death Penalty
and
The Capital Punishment Project, American Civil Liberties Union
132 West 43rd Street
New York, N.Y. 10036
These are two separate organizations that operate out of the same office building. The National Coalition numbers some fifty organizations among its members and is a good source of information about state coalitions in opposition to the death penalty.

NAACP Legal Defense Fund
10 Columbus Circle
New York, N.Y. 10019
The Legal Defense Fund has for years been in the forefront of litigation opposing the death penalty. Its New York office keeps abreast of all capital punishment trials and cases throughout the country.

Southern Coalition on Jails and Prisons
P.O. Box 12044
Nashville, Tennessee 37212
The Southern Coalition is a region-wide organization for prison and jail reform and opposed to the death penalty. It has an office in every southern state and is an excellent source of information about death penalty matters in the South.

Fellowship of Reconciliation
Box 271
Nyack, N.Y. 10906

Long a peace activist organization, the Fellowship has available by mail many articles and books on capital punishment as well as posters and the well-known abolitionist button, "Why do we kill people who kill people to show that killing people is wrong?"

Amnesty International, U.S.A.
304 W. 58th Street
New York, N.Y. 10019
Known for its world-wide work to free political prisoners and prisoners of conscience, Amnesty opposes the death penalty in all countries. It has local chapters throughout the country and has published a survey of the state of capital punishment around the world.

Work Group on the Death Penalty
National Interreligious Task Force on Criminal Justice
475 Riverside Drive, Room 1700-A
New York, N.Y. 10027
This work group brings together many people and resources from the major denominations and is an excellent source of information about the death penalty in general and also about church opposition to capital punishment.

# Appendix B      Bibliography

Literature on the death penalty varies from rigorous, technical studies written by social scientists to memoirs of prison chaplains. I have included here only a very small portion of the books and articles available. In my research I found these materials the most helpful.

*Sentenced to Die, The People, the Crimes and the Controversy*
by Stephen H. Gettinger
   Macmillan, 1979
(an excellent overview of death penalty questions seen through eight separate cases)

*The Death Penalty in America*
by Hugo A. Bedau
   Aldine, 1967

*Capital Punishment*
ed. by T. Sellin
   Harper and Row, 1967

*Capital Punishment: The Inevitability of Caprice and Mistake*
by Charles L. Black Jr.
   W.W. Norton and Company Inc. 1974

*Executions in America*
by William J. Bowers
   D.C. Heath and Co. 1974

*Cruel and Unusual: The Supreme Court and Capital Punishment*
by Michael Meltsner
   William Morrow and Co. 1974

"Death by Decree"
by Colin Turnbull
*Natural History,* May 1978

*engage/social action* numbers 30 and 58
100 Maryland Avenue, N.E.
Washington, D.C. 20002

"Will He Be First"
by Peter Ross Range

*New York Times Magazine,* March 11, 1979
(reprints available from the Fellowship of Reconciliation, see
Appendix A)

*For Capital Punishment: Crime and the Morality of the Death
Penalty*
by Walter Berns
  Basic Books, 1979

"License to Kill"
by Graham Hughes
*New York Review of Books,* June 28, 1979

# Acknowledgments

This book is the result of a collaboration. My collaborators, of course, are the men and women who agreed to talk to me and to have their private lives exposed in print. Through all the problems of editing and writing this book I have not forgotten that the work was made possible because people who were sentenced to die responded to a stranger's request that they share difficult, painful, sometimes horrible parts of their lives with the rest of us.

My introduction to these people came through the kindness and concern of people in many quarters. The following death row inmates, corrections officials, lawyers; abolitionists and friends have my grateful thanks for their suggestions, stories, criticisms and support: John Adams, Jack Boger, Kathy Bradford, John Brown, Dick Burr, Susan Cary, John Carroll, Robert Childress, Larry Cox, Willie Darden, Murphy Davis, Morris Dees, Randy Dempsey, L.C. Dorsey, John Foreman, Tom Gardner, Nancy Goodwin, Ann Gordon, Tom Gregory, William Groseclose, Mary Ellen Haines, John Hale, Andy Hall, David Hinkley, Robert Hoyt, Scharlette Holdman, Jerry Wayne Jacobs, Mike Jendrzejczyk, Jenny Johnston, Paul Jordan, Ellen Levitov, Ed Loring, John Lozier, Tim McCorquodale, Alan McGregor, Robert Mance III, Billy Moore, George Moore, Jim Murphy, Ray and Debby Nance, Pam Nelson, Mary Ann Oakley, Joe Oliver, Carol Palmer, Sarah Passmore, Peter Range, Carolyn Robinson, Henry Schwarzschild, Cardell Spaulding, Bill Stanton, Bob Sullivan, Michael Sullivan, John Vodicka, Randy Volkell, Johnny Washington, Charles Wenninger, San and Jan Williams, Harmon Wray.

A special thanks to Liz Hogan for her transcriptions of the tapes and her encouragement. And to Jeff Weber and Mimi Houston for their support and typewriter.

Joe Ingle put me on the road to this book both directly by introducing me to John Spenkelink and indirectly by the example of his own work.

Dick Pollard of *Us* magazine first gave me the opportunity to walk on to death row. Paul Sherry helped me see that the work I was doing should be made available in book form.

Finally I'd like to thank Esther Cohen for her care and her patience.

And Timmy Magee, someday I hope you understand why we couldn't play ball as much as you would have liked these past nine months.